MORE THAN A PROMISE

Exploring our covenant relationship with God

Arnell Motz

AlethinosBooks

© 2014 H. Arnell Motz

Published by Alethinos Books,
            San Diego, CA 92115

Printed in the United States of America
            Epic Print Solutions, Tempe, AZ

Library of Congress Cataloging-in-Publication Data

Motz, H. Arnell.
        More Than a Promise
        Summary: exploring our covenant relationship with God

    ISBN- 0-9779869-4-2
    BT155.M798 2014
    231.7 – 83-21408

Cover design by former Ron Youngblood student, Scott Wildey

Editor: Phil Corr, PhD

Editorial reading: Cliff Anderson, EdD; Marline Pallais; Terri Motz

In Memory of

Ronald F. Youngblood, PhD

CONTENTS

FOREWORD

We don't hear the word "covenant" a lot these days. It sounds rather odd and old fashion to most people. A Google search of the word brings up almost exclusively religious websites or else institutions like hospitals and schools that once had religious affiliations.

This is truly a shame, since the world today needs to know this word. A covenant is a commitment motivated by love. When I married my wife I established a covenant with her, promising to love and cherish her, for better for worse, for richer or for poorer, in sick and in health, till death we would part. I have committed myself to remain faithful to this covenant. As human beings, we sometimes fall short in our commitments. Yet God in his perfection never fails in his covenant relationships.

When God created human beings in his own image, he established a covenant relationship with them. In love, he promised to provide for their needs and to be faithful to them. Their responsibility was to love and serve him, and to obey his commands. Human beings, however, chose to reject God's covenant and go their own way. This was disastrous and would have been the end of the human race, except that God, because of his perfect love and covenant faithfulness, launched a rescue plan to renew this relationship.

In this volume Arnell Motz expertly explores the meaning of the biblical covenants. He shows through textual analysis and personal anecdotes how the concept of covenant is central to the biblical story and at the heart of the Gospel message. God's commitment to us is evident in his covenant faithfulness, which in turn motivates and empowers us to be faithful to him and faithful to one another.

This volume is a helpful guide for anyone interested in this important biblical theme. Yet it is also a delight for me to endorse because it was inspired by the life and teachings of our dear friend and mentor Ron Youngblood. I met Ron as a young scholar, wet behind the ears and just out of doctoral work. I had just been hired to teach New Testament at Bethel Seminary in San Diego. As a seasoned Old Testament scholar, Ron was incredibly kind and generous. Although his biblical knowledge and teaching skills were legendary, Ron was a humble man who always sought the best in others. He was a great mentor for me and a model for what it means to walk in covenant relationship with God and with others.

I hope you will read this book for what it is, a labor of love intended to encourage and uplift the church. Read it as a devotional guide to examine your own covenant relationship with God and to discover what it means to walk more faithfully with him.

Mark L. Strauss

INTRODUCTION

Ron Youngblood, PhD – born in 1931, lived a full adventurous life and died July 5, 2014. Some will remember him as an Old Testament scholar, Bethel professor, author of numerous books, translator for the NIV Bible, chairman of the board of the International Bible Society. I will remember him as friend. I will remember his welcoming nudge every Monday to join what I called the "patriarch's lunch" at Burger King near the seminary as they solved the world's problems or passed out articles from various theological journals.

This book is dedicated to the memory of Ron Youngblood who was one of the last to read the manuscript and make editorial contributions. I can hear Ron saying with enthusiasm in his voice, "Covenant is one of my favorite themes." This is the reason you will encounter frequent references to Ron's writing on covenants.

The purpose for the book is to help us ponder what I consider one of the most important concepts if we are to understand our relationship with God. The second purpose is to honor a friend who made a significant impact on the lives of our students and those who knew him.

My personal wrestling with this idea of covenant relationship came after my wife, son and I had just returned from missionary service in Bolivia and before that in Ethiopia. In terms of North American living conditions, I expected that life would be easier. But such was not the case. Suddenly we were hit with a number of crisis points that took me to the depths of despair. However, there was one anchor point that I would hang on to keep me going, namely my covenant relationship with God.

In my Baptist background if you asked, "What does it mean to have a covenant relationship with God?" I might hear one of two reactions. Some would become suspicious of a dissimilar theological agenda while others would dismiss it as a topic only applying to ancient Israel. My desire is that this book would help all of us discover one of the most neglected teachings of Scripture and yet one of the most enriching truths for living the Christian life.

Why has it been neglected? Because there has been a great divide in evangelical circles between covenant theology and dispensational theology. Any discussion of the concept of covenant relationship would be seen as forcing the agenda of either position. Instead of talking about why God even used covenant-making in his relationship with his people, we slip into arguments around infant baptism and whether the church replaces Israel in our eschatology. So we avoid the argument by neglecting the teaching.

What a tragedy! The attempt of this study is to help you explore the richness of what it means to have a covenant relationship with God. I will attempt a brief explanation of the issues that divide our theologies. However, my desire is to explore the foundational teaching of covenant relationship in Scripture so that all believers can be deepened in their own personal walk with God. I believe that can happen when we are overwhelmed with what it means to have a God who commits himself to us.

Thus the title – *More Than A Promise*. To grasp the importance of covenant-making one must realize that this goes beyond making a promise. We often in a flippant way say, "I promise ..." Sometimes we make promises for things we cannot control. When God makes a covenant it is *more than a promise*. It is a commitment that is rooted in the very nature of God.

J. I. Packer contends that covenant is not only the scenery that decorates the biblical narrative, but a hermeneutic which gives clarity to the metanarrative. It is the concept of commitment in covenant-making that is key for understanding all of Scripture.

To explore what that commitment means, there are questions at the end of each chapter that can be used for personal study or small group discussion.

By design the presentation in each chapter is meant to be brief and to be devotional in nature so as to facilitate small group interaction or a personal journey of discovery. Use your concordance or online Bible search to explore themes presented in each chapter. The concept of covenant relationship is woven throughout the entire written Word. It is the "metanarrative" – the big picture of what God is doing throughout history.

Search for it as you would a buried treasure and when you find it, delight in its beauty and richness. It will be like a diamond. A cursory reading could make it seem like a chip of glass. A thoughtful study will bring out its intricate beauty when held up to the Light and all of his glory (John 1:1-14).

Arnell Motz

1

WHO NEEDS A COVENANT

Can you remember the song "All You Need Is Love"? It was written by John Lennon and first performed by The Beatles on *Our World*. It was the first live global television link and was broadcast to 26 countries watched by 400 million people. That was June 25, 1967.

So what has happened to love since the song was released? Did this express the pinnacle of "love" in our world? Has our world been changed because the virtue of love has been given center stage? I think most would say that we are far from it. Ethnic conflicts in our world have continued to increase. Sexual love has become the defining characteristic of relationships in our culture, but do people feel more loved because of it? Even in our Christian circles love is often expressed with selfish motives, such as what can I get for my personal needs rather than what can I give to meet the needs of others? If you have bought into the idea that "all you need is love" then you have been cheated. Love without a context of commitment is empty and egocentric. That is true of marriage. And that is particularly true of our spiritual lives.

If this description has caught your attention, then maybe it is time to look at relationships through a different lens. Maybe it is time to look through the lens of God's covenant relationship and see that it changes how you experience love: the kind of love that God gives and the kind that will change you from the inside out.

Who needs a covenant relationship? You do. We all do. If we were capable of looking at our lives from God's perspective we would see that nothing works (especially love) unless there is a commitment between the two parties that transcends the context of our relationship. Commitment is the whole point of God's covenant-making.

Our Self-Centered World

Our nature is so self-centered. "What's in it for me?" is the guiding principle of our relationships. It reflects our sinful nature which will always leave our expressions of love incomplete. When we meet a special someone we want to marry, we pledge our love will be forever. But most couples would admit that within a year or two of marriage the passion has cooled and our view of the other person has changed. Her cute little ways of doing things become annoying, and the admiration of his firmness when making decisions is now viewed as irritating stubbornness. Love changed in how it was viewed or felt because when we think of love, our thinking begins with "me."

That can be said of other relationships too. Even our love for God is always victim to anemia. Where once it burned with a passion to know Christ, it can now experience that tired, run-down feeling, and be in need of renewing and revitalizing. We all are affected by standards and values of the world in which we live. Jesus even warned that "because of the increase of wickedness the love of most will grow cold" (Matt 24:12). That was his warning for the last days before his return, but I need to ask: How do I guard my love for Christ from suffering this kind of apathy? I believe it takes a renewing of our vision of God and a change of thinking about relationship with God.

Exploring the significance of a covenant-making God paints for us the big picture of his persevering love. The concept of "covenant" expresses something more than a promise, as important as his promises are. It expresses commitment: the context in which love is fully known.

We all admit that by nature we are self-centered. In contrast, we are called to be Christ-centered. Making Christ the center of our lives transforms the quality of who we are and how we experience God.

Some might respond, "I know that, but I still feel something is lacking. I need a self-help book for spiritual doldrums. I need some spiritual experience that would fix the way I feel about God and about life."

I can identify with feelings of spiritual anemia. After being a Christian for 50 plus years and serving as a missionary for 25 years I should have this figured out. But I too have my struggles. A few years ago I went through two of the darkest years of my life. Psalm 77 described what I was going through—my soul refusing to be comforted, feeling rejected by God, questioning his promises, so troubled I couldn't sleep. I felt abandoned. My prayer time was focused on pleading with God to rescue me. I was stuck in the quagmire of depression.

That is how I felt, but what was the reality? Had God abandoned me? Was I really alone in these struggles that I was going through? Was the stress I was under any worse than what Moses felt as he fled for his life from Pharaoh; or David felt when his own men wanted to stone him? No, I had simply lost sight of the big picture of what God wanted to do because of his committed relationship with me.

The Big Picture

The fact is, *all* of God's revelation—from the beginning to the end of the Bible—reassures me that he has not abandoned me. I may feel alone in my struggles, but he is constantly affirming, "I will be with you." How does he assure me? He pictures through his revealed word key concepts that remind me of his commitment to me and *to be with* me. One of those concepts described in the Bible is what is termed "covenant."

There are three key concepts that affect my relationship with God. They are so important that God communicates these in word pictures:

- sacrifice
- adoption
- covenant

In the word "sacrifice" you can picture taking the life of an animal as a sacrifice for sin: either on a stone altar or on the altar of burnt offering in the temple court. The key concept being pictured is one of forgiveness or atonement for sins. It communicates what is essential in order to be accepted by a holy God.

When Adam and Eve sinned by eating of the fruit of the tree of the knowledge of good and evil, death was the penalty. But God, because of his great mercy, provided a substitutionary sacrifice that was pictured in the animal sacrifice for sins. This becomes the basis of God restoring a relationship that was established in creation.

In the word "adoption" you can picture a child of slavery being adopted into the family of a rich landowner so that the child has all the rights and privileges of a natural born child. The Bible uses this picture to help us understand the kind of relationship we enjoy with God. We deserved nothing, yet in his grace he lavished on us everything. We were adopted into his royal family and given the status of "heirs with Christ" (Rom. 8:17). This expresses the strength of commitment in our relationship.

What about the word "covenant"? Jesus used this term in instituting the celebration of the Lord's Supper. He said: "This cup is the new covenant in my blood; do this in remembrance of me" (1 Cor. 11:25). Why is the covenant picture so important? It is because the idea of covenant pictures a relationship of commitment, the kind of commitment that only God can show because of his infinite love for us. It is the kind of commitment he desires from us because we are loved by God.

Why is this vital to your spiritual health? Growing in your relationship with God will have many obstacles that covenant relationship will help us overcome. One common problem most of us experience is having a sense of inferiority. We compare ourselves to people around us which leads to feeling our lack of value. We then take the next step to think that maybe God does not see value in us either.

Sometimes our memory of past failures and sins haunts us with a sense of shame and we think that God may have given up on us, or passed us over for someone more deserving. As a result, our relationship with God seems shallow and empty of meaning. That is why we need to look again at the strength conveyed through God's covenant-making, and why God knew we needed a covenant.

Experiencing God

Most of what we refer to as the "old covenant" with its sacrificial system and symbols of God's presence comes to us through the life and writings of Moses. Personally, if I was Moses and I had to choose between God communicating through a word picture or God actually speaking through a burning bush, I would chose the burning bush. Would not that be easier to understand? Why could not God always lead with a burning bush experience where he simply gave me a roadmap for my life, where all the important decisions were told to me rather than wanting to lead me in some mystical process of hearing and obeying?

The reason God uses a process of 'leading' rather than 'dictating' is because he is more concerned with *being* than with *doing*. He is more interested with our knowing him in his holiness and being the kind of person who listens to his voice than in doing the kind of activities that we think should generate 'burning bush experiences.' On occasion he may use a burning bush, but God desires a relationship that transforms us from the inside out and leads us from his voice within. It is a relationship of experiencing God.

That is why we need this picture of commitment that covenant relationship gives us. It helps us discover what it means to have a special relationship with God where our focus is not a burning bush but a "still small voice." And in that relationship our desire is *being* the kind of person who can hear that voice.

This is the tipping point of our spiritual life. It is our understanding and experiencing God that changes who we are so that we can be the kind of person he can use. It is the process of listening and obeying that changes our *being* so that he can put us in a place of *doing* according to his kingdom purpose.

Application of covenant relationship

David reflects on this relationship in Psalm 103. His relationship with God was revived as he reminded himself of the benefits that came to him through this covenant relationship – "who forgives all your sins" (v.3), "who redeems your life from the pit and crowns you with love *(hesed)* and compassion" (v.4). David reflects on God's *hesed* [1], his covenant-making love (a term we will examine later in this study) which he describes as a love that is "from everlasting to everlasting" (v.17). Because of this love, he does not "treat us as our sins deserve" (v.10) but overflows with lovingkindness and mercy to us. He freely gives us what we do not deserve.

David reminds himself and his reader of what it means to keep God's covenant (v.18), to obey his word (v.20), and do his will (v.21). It was a commitment of being completely devoted to him. But what about those times when we have failed in our devotion to him? What if we are feeling worthless because of past sins?

His covenant should remind us that "as far as the east is from the west, so far has he removed our transgressions from us" (v.12). What if we are feeling a lack of self-worth? David says, "He remembers that we are but dust" (v.14). God knows what we are made of (he has realistic expectations of us even when we do not) and he has compassion on us because we are his children (v.13). Do you want to be renewed in your spirit and your devotion to God? Then bask again in what it means to have a relationship with a covenant-making God.

---

[1] Andrew Hill and John Walton, *A Survey of the Old Testament.* p. 25, 253
Merrill Unger and William White, (ed.) *Nelson's Expository Dictionary of the Old Testament.* p. 232
(Unger and White transliterates חמד as *chesed* while Hill and Walton use *hesed*)

Covenant relationship brings transformation

Today the desire for God to do something new in our lives captures our attention. We wonder what could be missing in our spiritual experience that God has for us as individual believers. Is there some external experience that would bring personal revival?

One of the most important theological truths for personal revival is how God expresses his relationship to us through what Scripture calls a covenant. Ron Youngblood suggests that "the concept of covenant is the most fundamental and overarching idea in the entire Bible."[2] Andrew Murray writes:

> To many a man, who has never been taught about the Covenant, a true and living faith in it would mean the transformation of his whole life...[3] I am persuaded that nothing will help us more in our work of intercession than the entrance for ourselves personally into what it means that we have a covenant God.[4]

Though written over a century ago, the above quotation is true today. We sometimes look for something more spectacular to call us to spiritual vitality and devotion to God, but getting a hold on what it means to have a covenant-making God will strengthen our desire to be committed to him. When we see how devoted God is to us we will want to be devoted to him.

Observing the very nature of God through the lens of covenant relationship will help us better understand the heart of God. What compels the creator of the

---

[2] Ronald Youngblood, *The Heart of the Old Testament*, p.38.
[3] Andrew Murray, *The Believer's New Covenant*, p.13.
[4] Murray, p.10.

universe to even care about the lives of us mere mortals? I do not know, but he does. The psalmist says:

> Though the Lord is on high he looks upon the lowly.
> Though I walk in the midst of trouble you preserve my life.   (Psalm 138:6-7)

I ask, "How high?" Answer, "As high as a universe with 10,000 million galaxies each containing billions of stars."[5] And then I ask, "How low?" Answer, "As low as my inadequacies." Yet he cares about me. He looks upon me and holds my hand. Why? Because of his character and nature that are revealed through his covenant-making.   And through this lens I better understand God.

Take a look at some of the implications this has for you. Be open to the Holy Spirit's work of transforming you. I believe that Andrew Murray's promise is true: "nothing will help us more than to enter into what it means to have a covenant relationship with God."

---

[5] http://en.wikipedia.org/wiki/Univer

Study Questions:

Read Exodus 3 –

1. What characteristics or aspects of God did he reveal
    about himself in the burning bush encounter with
    Moses?

2. Which of these characteristics of God relate to God's
    covenant-making?

3. From your understanding of Scripture, how have
    the concepts of sacrifice, adoption, and covenant
    impacted your relationship with God? Can you
    think of a verse for each concept that stresses its
    importance?

Read Psalm 77 –

4. What characteristics of God described in Psalm 77
    reflect on his commitment to us? How should that
    help us get through our times of deep distress?

Praying the thoughts of Psalm 103 –

5. Lay Psalm 103 open before you and express
    through prayer those thoughts that stand out to
    you about your 'covenant relationship' with God.

2

WHY GOD MAKES A COVENANT

The first question that we need to answer is: "why a covenant?" Why does God choose to make a covenant? Why does he not do what he wants to do when he wants to do it? He is omnipotent. He could act on whatever whim he might have. The answer is simple: it is because *love obligates*. That is the nature of true love. God, because of his very nature, makes a covenant with mankind whereby he obligates himself to us because "God is love."

To understand this, think about marriage as a covenant relationship. Malachi 2:14 refers to our "marriage covenant." It can help us understand how love obligates. What if I said, "Let's do away with the institution of marriage. In our culture it is quite common for people to just live together. Marriage is an old fashioned concept. Let's just remove it from our civil code and be free to live with whoever and whenever you feel like it. Should not the highest expression of love be free love?"

Even if you were to pretend that there were no biblical or legal reasons for marriage would you still want a marriage covenant? Yes, of course you would!

That is because if you really love someone you want to commit yourself exclusively to that person and you want that person to show exclusive love to you.

The highest form of love compels you to obligate yourself. So then God who loves to the greatest degree and fullest measure possible uses a covenant to obligate himself to us.

God's Purpose

At creation there was a covenant relationship. Adam and Eve could talk with God in the garden. They did not have a formally instituted covenant as the ones God established after the Fall, but Adam and Eve enjoyed a covenant relationship with God.

The first time the word "covenant" is found in the Bible it is used with Noah (Gen. 6:18). But in the book of Hosea, God refers to Adam and Eve breaking a 'creation covenant.' Hosea 6:7 says: "Like Adam, they have broken the covenant; they were unfaithful to me there."

The basic terms of the covenant: not to eat the fruit of the tree of knowledge of good and evil in the center of the garden. They were to have faith that God would provide what was good for them, and in doing that, they would know him and have fellowship with him.

With the fall of man came a loss of that relationship with God. God then entered into a covenant-making relationship with the human race whereby God would obligate himself to mankind and they would obligate themselves to God. The twofold purpose was to:

(1) *restore relationship* with God, and
(2) call for *complete devotion* to God.

This purpose is best expressed in the covenant formula repeated throughout Scripture. We first read it in Genesis 17 and the last reference is Revelation 21, from the Garden of Eden to the New Jerusalem. Sometimes the order is reversed but both ideas are presented:

"I will be their God and they will be my people."

God desires that we would be a people completely devoted to him, so he enacts a covenant relationship in which he is completely devoted to us.

Through his covenant with Abraham, he forms a people or nation that he calls his "chosen people" (Is. 65:9). As we will see when we look at the individual covenants, God will use this people to bring his Messiah to all mankind and through him to bless all peoples of the earth. Under the New Covenant his people are called 'the church' or the 'body of Christ.' It now includes not only the Jewish nation but all nations (1 Pet. 2:4). When God brings history to its final chapter, Revelation 7 describes this people as "a great multitude that no one could count, from every nation, tribe, people, and language, standing before the throne and in front of the Lamb" (v.9).

To be *his people* is to be marked as a people with a special relationship with the Lord God of the universe. He did not create mankind and then step back to see what would happen. He did not create us for some impersonal relationship, but rather for the most personal relationship possible. That is because God desires a people who would be special to him and he would love them as *his people*.

Amazing Love Story

God's devotion to us as his people is pictured in the book of Hosea in an unusual story of God's amazing love. What happens when God's people forget their commitment to their God, when like Adam they are unfaithful to his covenant relationship? Does God abandon them as we do in our relationships? No. God implements a plan of redemption and then calls his people back into relationship by demonstrating his amazing love.

I can think of no other story in the Old Testament that better pictures this than the account of Hosea and Gomer. God wants to illustrate to Israel what it feels like when his people are unfaithful to him in their covenant relationship. He also wants to demonstrate the extent to which he is willing to go to call them back into relationship. To do this he tells his prophet, Hosea, to marry a prostitute named Gomer. It would be like God telling your pastor to marry a prostitute. That would be pretty shocking, but God wanted an object lesson that would shock his people into renewing their relationship with him.

God tells Hosea, "Go, take to yourself an adulterous wife and children of unfaithfulness, because the land is guilty of the vilest adultery in departing from the Lord" (Hosea 1:2).

So that is what Hosea does. He marries Gomer and has children with her. The first child was a son. God said to name him 'Jezreel' (1:4) as a reminder of the sin of "the house of Jehu for the massacre at Jezreel." It was a reminder of Israel's unfaithfulness.

Their second child was a daughter named 'Lo-Ruhamah' which means "not loved" in that God would judge by withholding his love from Israel but show his love to Judah.

After Lo-Ruhamah Gomer gives birth to a third child, a son who God says to name 'Lo-Ammi' meaning "not my people" (1:8). God uses this to describe the condition of how they were living towards God—"for you are not my people and I am not your God." Was

God saying that they would no longer be his people? No. Because he goes on to say, "In the place where it was said to them, 'You are not my people' they will be called 'sons of the living God.'" It is the heart of God to call out to his people as "my people" and to say, "My loved one." (1:10- 2:1)

How does God picture his love to his people? He brings the lesson down to our level by using Gomer's unfaithfulness to Hosea. It seems from the biblical account that in spite of Hosea's love for her, she wanders off into her old promiscuous lifestyle. She sneaks out of her home to find herself in one man's arms and then another; into their beds in search of love but coming up empty. To make it worse, the story implies that with each man she goes into a downward spiral of abuse and neglect where these lovers no longer care for her basic needs.

How does Hosea respond? He searches for her to provide for her needs. She has abandoned her husband, her children, and deserves nothing in any form of kindness, yet that is what Hosea shows to her. He brings her grain, new wine and oil, even gold and silver to buy what she needs. Why would he do such a thing? So that she would say, "I will go back to my husband as at first, for then I was better off than now." (2:7)

However, Gomer does not respond in repentance or desire for her husband, causing Hosea to take the opposite approach. He stopped giving her the supplies, the wool and linen "intended to cover her nakedness. So now I will expose her lewdness before the eyes of her lovers" (2:10).

Is she now ready to respond to Hosea's love? The word of the Lord to Hosea is, "Go show your love to your wife again, though she is loved by another and is an adulteress." (3:1) How does he win her back? By redeeming her from the auction block at the slave market. In those days it was common to have slaves sold like merchandise and to stand naked for the auctioneer to sell to the buyers. Such seemed to be the fate of Gomer.

Maybe a voice yells out, "I'll pay seven shekels of silver." Someone else counters, "I'll pay 10." "The first replies, "15 shekels of silver." A male slave would fetch about 30 pieces of silver. A woman, a well-used woman should be worth about 15. But then another voice yells out, "15 shekels and a homer of barley." It seems too much for this piece of flesh, but in that quiet pause of the crowd waiting for the auctioneer to end this, Hosea cries out, "I'll give you 15 shekels of silver and a homer-and-a-half of barley." There is a quiet gasp from the crowd, and Gomer is declared "sold."

Will Gomer now face the consequences of her choices? Will Hosea keep her as a slave since she had decided to not be his wife? No. Hosea redeemed her from the auction block of her sin so that he could say to her, "I will betroth you to me forever; I will betroth you in righteousness and justice, in love and compassion. I will betroth you in faithfulness and you will acknowledge the Lord." (2:19-20)

That is exactly what God wanted to say to Israel, his chosen people. He was saying "to those called 'Not my people,' 'You are my people'; so that they would say, 'You are my God.'" (2:23)

What about us?

The story reminds us that we are the ones on the auction block of sin. We need to be redeemed and loved as Gomer was loved. That is what Christ did for us. With his own blood he purchased us, all because of his amazing love. The Apostle Paul takes it a step further when he writes to the Corinthians – "You are not your own; you have been bought at a price. Therefore glorify God with your bodies" (1 Cor. 6:20).

Being overwhelmed with what Christ did for us helps us realize that we belong to him and makes us feel privileged that he would even want to claim us as *his people* (term of designation more than description).

The story of Hosea also shows us that God does whatever it takes to show his love and to bring us into a relationship as *his people*. In Hosea 5:15 God says, "In their misery they will seek me." Sometimes God's love is a tough love. He allows us to go through times of misery, hard times that are for our good, because they help us seek the Lord. In the words of Hosea 10:12, "Break up the unploughed ground for it is time to seek the Lord."

To be *his people* is to want to seek the Lord even when the ground becomes hard. How does it get that way? Is it because we become so accustomed to spiritual junk in our lives that we lose the desire to seek the Lord?

God proclaims the way he prefers to lead us in Hosea 11:4, "I led them with cords of human kindness, with ties of love." In 14:4 he says – "I will heal their waywardness and love them freely." Being *his people* is to be the object of his love, whether it is experienced as tough love or the love of human kindness.

Being *his people* also means that nothing can separate us from the love of God. Romans 8:39 reminds us of that. When going through times of trouble or hardship or danger we may wonder if God still loves us. But in those times we are assured that "neither death nor life, neither angels or demons, neither the present nor the future... nor anything else in all creation will be able to separate us from the love of God that is in

Christ Jesus our Lord." That is his commitment to us as his people.

Covenant Formula

Why does God make a covenant? It is because the nature of God is to love and to love us with a self-giving love or *agapé* love. True love obligates, not to earn love but to show love. In a covenant, God obligates himself to us to be our God and calls for commitment from us to be his people. God wants a people who will say to him, "You will be our God, and we will be your people."

That is the second reason for covenant-making: to have a people who are completely devoted to him. God desires a people who love him with all of our heart and soul and strength (Deut. 6:4). That is what it means to be his people.

All of these truths are wrapped in a simple package which we call the 'covenant formula.' As we have already said, it reminds us that the purpose of God's covenant-making is to:

- restore relationship
  - *I will be their God*
- call for complete devotion
  - *they will be my people*

Andrew Murray, emphasizing the same idea, has said:

> The Covenant was meant to be a *security and guarantee*, as simple and understandable as the divine glory could make it, that the very things which God had promised would indeed be brought to pass and worked out with whom He had entered into Covenant... And so the Covenant was, above all, to give man *a hold upon God*, as the Covenant-keeping God, to link him to God himself in expectation and

hope, to bring him to make God himself alone the portion and the strength of his soul.[1]

We all need to have a sense of laying hold of God. When we are overcome with feelings of aloneness and being abandoned by God we need to be overwhelmed with his amazing love and his strong commitment to us. When we lay hold of the God who is for us, we will respond with expressions of devotion. When we are lured by temptations that take us away from God, his love will draw us back to that restored relationship with God and desire to live in complete devotion to God.

In Romans 9 Paul cites the Hosea lesson about Israel to show that *my people* now includes the Gentiles. Under the new covenant they have the privilege of being grafted in because God desires from all nations a people who will say, "You will be my God and I will be your people."

We hear the same reminders in 2 Corinthians 6 and Hebrews 8. But then Revelation 21 describes the final scene of history where we are with Christ in the New Jerusalem. In the climax of what it means to be with his people John writes, "He will live with them. They will be his people, and God himself will be with them and be their God. He will wipe away every tear from our eyes. There will be no more death or mourning or crying or pain, for the old order of things has passed away. " (vv. 3-4)

The covenant formula reminds us both of our final relationship with Christ but also of the privilege of living in that relationship now – as God's people!

---

[1] Andrew Murray, *The Believer's New Covenant.* p. 15.

Study Questions:

Read Genesis 12:1-3

1. Where do you get your greatest sense of belonging? From a society club, family, work, military unit? What is distinctive about being *his people* that should give us our sense of worth or belonging?

Read Hosea 1 to 3

2. What were the unusual measures God used in this story of Hosea and why should these help Israel to be faithful to his covenant?

3. What reminders does this account have for us today?

Praying a verse of Scripture –

4. Select from the following references and pray a response for what it reminds us of in our relationship to God.

Gen. 17:7	Lev. 26:12	
Jer. 11:4	Jer. 31:33	Jer. 32:38
Ez. 11:20	Ez. 34:30	Ez. 37:27
Hosea 2:23	Zech. 8:8	
2 Cor. 6:16	Heb. 8:10-12	Rev. 21:3-7

3

WHAT IS A COVENANT

In our culture today we rarely use the word covenant. Maybe it is because we shy away from anything which might obligate us or involve a long-term commitment. When we do make a covenant—such as with a contract for buying something very expensive—it usually involves lawyers because we want to ensure the other person will be bound to the terms of the covenant.

The word *covenant* in the culture of the Old Testament had many uses. There is a marital use in Malachi 2:14 and a political use in 1 Kings 5:12. But the most prevalent use in Scripture is a redemptive use. Ron Youngblood defines covenant as: "A formal agreement between God and man which possesses legal validity and which is eternally operative."[1]

Youngblood drew upon the culture of that day to emphasize the biblical nature of covenant-making. It required a commitment that was legally binding so that it required faithfulness. It also was redemptive in terms of God's eternal purposes.

---

[1] Ron Youngblood, *The Heart of the Old Testament,* p.38.

Using archaeological research of the past century to give us the cultural setting, Youngblood relates how a French expedition in 1933 excavated the old Amorite city of Mari on the Euphrates River. Thousands of clay documents were unearthed that described life in Mesopotamia during the eighteenth century B.C. Several Mari letters told about the practice of sacrificing a donkey as a means to confirm an oath of alliance between two peoples or nations.

Youngblood also describes how the Hittites signed parity and suzerainty treaties or covenants with the nations on their borders. He defines a parity treaty as a "covenant that was consummated between equals." A suzerainty treaty was one "where the vassal ruler and his subjects would have nothing to say about the stipulations of the covenant but would be compelled to submit to the demands of the Hittite suzerain."[2] It is interesting to note that in biblical descriptions of covenants the relationships between the covenant parties "are never established on the basis of parity. God and his creatures do not come to the conference table as equals. The Lord of the universe does not abdicate his position of sovereignty when he enters into solemn agreements with his people."[3]

Meaning of 'Covenant'

In the Old Testament the Hebrew word used for covenant is *berith*, used about 260 times. It most probably comes from the Akkadian root meaning "to fetter.'[4] It is the idea of something that is binding.

---

[2] Youngblood, p. 40.
[3] Ibd, p. 61.
[4] Merrill Unger and William White Jr., *Nelson's Expository Dictionary of the Old Testament*, p. 82.

The most common verb used with *berith* is "to cut" (*karath*)[5] – meaning they "cut a covenant" which apparently comes from the ceremony described in Genesis 15 where it was witnessed with an animal sacrifice.

The English word covenant means "coming together," as in two parties coming together in mutual obligation. While living in Ethiopia, I saw a picture of this in their custom of making an agreement or contract. When a young man wanted to marry he would go to the father of the prospective bride and listen to the terms of what the suitor had to provide for his daughter. The two parties would agree to the terms with each having at least two elders (*shimagles* - Amharic) to witness the terms and then all participate in a meal sealing their obligation.

The New Testament uses the Greek word *diatheke* for covenant. It means "to make a disposition of one's own property." It is what we call a testament or will, as in when we die. However, there is another Greek word that could have been used – *syntheke* – which means a "contract." It was not used for covenant because this word implied equality on the part of the two parties in the contract. *Diatheke* was used in the Septuagint (the Greek translation of the Old Testament) for the Hebrew word *berith* because it signified an arrangement made by one party with plenary power. In other words, the other party can accept or reject the terms but they cannot alter the covenant.[6] The legal analogy is our making a will for our children. You have to die before it will take effect. They can accept it or walk away from it, but they cannot change it.

---

[5] Meredith Kline, *By Oath Consigned*, p. 14.
[6] *Baker's Dictionary of Theology*, p. 143-144.

Youngblood explains the one-party agreement by stating that biblical agreements are neither entirely one-sided nor is God the only active partner in his agreements with his people.

> God, who is perfectly righteous, sets the conditions of his covenants and brings them to his holiness, his justice, his grace and love. But God's people also have a part to play in the total relationship. Biblical covenants may be properly described as unilateral, then only to the extent that they are formulated by God and by him alone.[7]

What we call the "New Testament" is the word for "New Covenant." It is God's covenant with mankind fulfilled in Christ. When we read the New Testament portion of the Bible we are not merely reading later writings. Rather, we are hearing how God has fulfilled his obligation to us in the person of Christ. In our coming to Christ we accept or reject his terms in the agreement. We cannot alter or add to it, as some try to do. We come amazed at his grace that we are included in his covenant-making and in this relationship desire for him to fulfill his purpose in us.

To Cut a Covenant

To "cut a covenant" is pictured in Genesis 15:7-18 with God solemnizing his covenant with Abraham. In that day a covenant was made by both parties passing through the two halves of an animal sacrifice. They "cut a covenant" which had the sense of, "may it also be done to me if I do not keep this covenant."

In Genesis 15:4-5 God promises Abram (the pre-covenant name for Abraham) that: he will have an heir, his offspring will as numberless as the stars in the heavens, and he will take possession of this land God

---

[7] Youngblood, p. 42.

has brought him to. Abram replies: "How can I know that I will gain possession of it?" He is asking for some kind of surety or guarantee on a promise that is so big.

God tells Abram to prepare this culturally-based ceremony for solemnizing his covenant. Abram is to take a heifer, a goat and a ram, each three years old, along with a dove and a young pigeon. He then cuts the animals in two arranging the halves opposite each other. The birds are not cut but placed on each side as if making a path between the cut animals.

Usually the two parties walk between the halves with the idea of "cutting a covenant." But in this case God causes Abram to go into a deep sleep and then speaks his covenant after which God passes through the sacrifice as symbolized by the smoking firepot.

Why was it that only God passed through the sacrificed animals? It was because his covenant was based on God's faithfulness and God's alone.

Man demonstrated in the Fall that he could not keep a two-party agreement, so God's covenant with us is based on his ability to keep the covenant, not ours. There will be times when we will fail him. We will question whether God has given up on us. We might imagine him throwing up his hands in disgust saying, "You've failed me so many times that I've given up on you. You're hopeless." But God does not do that, even though we might deserve it. God instead obligates himself to us. He gives us a way to lay hold of God even in our unfaithfulness. He does this by making a covenant with us, based on his faithfulness alone.

Old and New Covenants

If the basis of God's covenant-making is his faithfulness, and the purpose is to restore relationship, then why does the book of Hebrews describe two separate covenants with the second, the New Covenant, said to be the "better covenant"? To be more specific, Hebrews 10:9 says: "He sets aside the first to establish the second." The writer then quotes Jeremiah 31:33 to show that this New Covenant was anticipated long ago. The promise, of what is making it unique, is that in this New Covenant "I will write my laws in their hearts and I will write them on their minds" (Heb. 10:16).

The comparison is made with the Old Covenant written on tablets of stone. It is an external code intended to test man's faithfulness. But man proved to be unfaithful. The New Covenant, in contrast, is promised to be an internal code, "written on their hearts." It is written "not with the letter that kills but with the Spirit who gives life" (2 Cor. 3:6).

One of the promises of the New Covenant is a different relationship with the Holy Spirit. In Isaiah 59:21 the Lord says: "This is my covenant with them. My Spirit who is *on* you..." The Spirit of God came on certain individuals for specific purposes. The Spirit was active in the Old Testament but in the New Covenant the Spirit begins his age of harvest. He is promised to be *in* the believer rather than *on* certain individuals. The relationship is now described as being more intimate, as adopted sons – "Because you are sons, God sent the Spirit of his Son into our hearts, the Spirit who calls out, 'Abba, Father'" (Gal. 4:6).

Paul writes in Romans 8 that "you did not receive a spirit that makes you a slave again to fear (i.e. Old Covenant), but you received the Spirit of sonship (i.e. New Covenant). And by him we cry, 'Abba, Father.' The Spirit himself testifies with our spirit that we are God's children" (Rom. 8:15-16). Paul goes on to describe the ministry the Spirit now has with us in this new relationship (8:26):

- The Spirit helps us in our weaknesses;
- The Spirit himself intercedes for us; and
- The Spirit searches our heart to bring conformity with God's will for us.

These are the promises that God gives to us, along with the assurance that God welcomes not only Israel into the New Covenant, but all peoples—Jew or Gentile, slave or free. All are made one in Christ and made heirs of the promise to Abraham (Gal. 3:29). James points this out to the Jerusalem Council in Acts 15:14 that God is "taking from the Gentiles a people for himself."

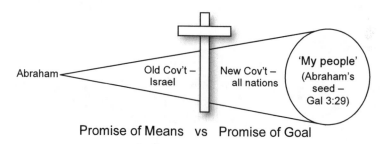

Promise of Means vs Promise of Goal

- Old – a nation with a promised land
- New – a bride of all nations

God gave the Old Covenant primarily to Israel as his chosen people. It was a promise of means. God demonstrates his holiness through his law and through his people. He promises blessings, some of which were conditional and some unconditional, but all to bring mankind to recognition of their need for a Redeemer and the subsequent response of crying out for mercy.

The Old Covenant "leads us to Christ" (Gal. 3:24) so that we would be "justified by faith." When Christ had been fully revealed (4:4), then we no longer needed the "supervision of the law" (3:25). He wrote his law on their hearts and minds. The New Covenant became the "better covenant" because it brought us into a new relationship of being "in Christ." It was a promise of goal – a promise that went beyond the nation of Israel to invite all nations to be "my people" (Heb. 7:22; 8:10).

As Andrew Murray writes:

> The (Old) Covenant ended in man proving his own unfaithfulness and failure. In the New Covenant, God is to prove what He can do with man, as unfaithful and feeble as he is, when He is allowed and trusted *to do all the work*. The Old Covenant was one dependent on man's obedience, one which he could break and did break (Jer. 31:32). The New Covenant was one which God has engaged and shall never be broken: He himself keeps it and ensures our keeping it, so He makes it an everlasting Covenant.[8] *[emphasis Murray]*

Living under his Covenant

Why did God need to use the concept of covenant for calling us into relationship with himself? God loves everyone in the world. Everyone should love God. We should be singing, "All you need is love."

But that is not the case. God uses the idea of covenant relationship because his love is based on commitment and faithfulness. He calls us to the same. Jokingly I used to advise young couples to "get married in the morning. That way if it doesn't work out, you won't have wasted a whole day." The failings of our human love are not a joke. Sometimes it is a painful reality because love breaks down at the point of our commitment and faithfulness.

Living under God's covenant is a glorious reminder of his commitment to us, and God always remains faithful to his commitments. There are also benefits of living under his covenant. We are promised a relationship with the Holy Spirit who lives in us. The Apostle Paul says, "your body is a temple of the Holy

---

[8] Murray, p.19.

Spirit who is in you" (1 Cor. 6:19). Under the Old Covenant the tabernacle and the temple were external symbols of God's presence. Under the New Covenant the symbol is internal. The Spirit lives in you and desires to control you. The Spirit promises to help you in your weaknesses, intercede for you in your praying to the Father, to conform your will to the will of God. Can anything be more amazing than that?

If the New Covenant is better, does that mean the Old was bad? No. The Old was good in that it brought us to the realization of our need for God's grace. It was good because it pictured how God wanted to come close to us, to *tabernacle* ("pitch a tent")[9] among us, to reveal himself in all of his holiness. It was good because it brought us to the place of complete dependence on God.

But the New is better because it brings us into a fuller relationship of being "*in* Christ." John describes this relationship as showing more of God's glory than when his tabernacle in the Old Covenant camped in the middle of the Israelites. John picks up this image in his gospel (1:14) and says:

> The Word became flesh and made his dwelling *('tabernacled')* among us. We have seen his glory, the glory of the One and Only, who came from the Father, full of grace and truth.

What is a covenant in God's terms? It is a reminder of how God binds himself to you in a special relationship of being *his people* and being *in Christ*, of his continuing faithfulness to you even when you have been unfaithful to him. It is God reminding you of the benefits and promises that are yours in this relationship. That should create a desire to be in a place of dependence on him, knowing that in that place he will show his glory.

---

[9] Marvin Vincent, *Word Studies in the New Testament*, p. 51.

Study Questions:

1. What are some of the advantages of making a will or final testament? What similarities do these have with God making a covenant?

2. Read Galatians 3:15-4:7.

   What are some of the advantages or benefits of the Old Covenant that Paul refers to? What is the significance of Paul saying we are now called "sons" and can call God "Abba Father"?

3. How would it affect our interpretation of "God's chosen people" (Israel) if we differentiate between the "promise of means" and the "promise of goal" in the Abrahamic covenant?

4. Think of yourself as someone in the nation of Israel who is going to the temple for worship and listening to Jeremiah prophecy about this "New Covenant" (Jer. 31:31-34). How would you have interpreted the promises in light of your situation in that time? How do you see them more fully from your perspective of today?

4

HOW GOD SHOWS RELATIONSHIP

What's in a name? Not much in our culture, but in other cultures such as in Africa, one's name has great significance. In Ethiopia everyone knows the meaning of their name. Rediet means 'blessing.' Tsehay means 'sunshine.' As for me, my parents choose my name, Arnell, because they liked the sound of it. They had no idea of origin or what it meant.

When our son was born we named him Jonathan because it means "gift of God." He was born with the umbilical cord wrapped around his neck and the doctor arrived at the hospital just in time to rescue him. His birth was a gift of God. I also wanted to say to him, "Your great grandfather's name was a German equivalent of Jonathan. He fled with his family under the cover of night from the 'old country' to live in freedom. Your name has a story."

When God chose his personal name it expressed something important. It told a story. In fact, God chose his covenant name to remind his people of his *covenant relationship* with them. To understand the significance of this, we shall look at some of the names used for God in Scripture.

In Psalm 91 the psalmist incorporates some of those names in this anthem of praise. In the first two verses he uses four names:

> He who dwells in the shelter of the *Most High*
> will rest in the shadow of the *Almighty*. I will say
> of the LORD, "He is my refuge and my fortress,
> my *God* in whom I trust."

El Elyon	- *God Most High*
El Shaddai	- *God Almighty*
YHWH	- *LORD (Jehovah)*
Elohim	- *God (general term for God)*

Most names for God are a combination of two names. The most often used Hebrew names are:

El: as a single word is used for "God" 250 times.

EL-ELYON: "Most High" (from "to go up").

EL-SHADDAI: "God Almighty" is used 48 times and conveys the picture of being awesome as a mighty mountain.

ELOHIM: "God" (a plural noun used with singular verbs) occurs 2,570 times to describe God as Creator, Preserver, Transcendent, and Strong.

EL-OLAM: "Everlasting God" (God of everlasting time).

ADONAI: "Lord" (using lower case o-r-d) has the idea of "Master" or "Lord." It is used 300 times in the Old Testament and is always plural when referring to God. It is singular when referring to a human lord.[1]

These names reminded the Israelite that in contrast to the gods of the nations around them, "there is no god like you." The Lord God is set apart from any other and he is to be worshipped in his "set-apartness."

---

[1] Unger and White, pp. 157-161.

Through His Covenant Name

To understand the nature of God one must begin with understanding his transcendence. God is all-powerful and above all. There is nothing that he cannot do. The names of El-Shaddai, El-Olam, El-Elyon, and Adonai remind us of who he is. Our God is a refuge and fortress because he is powerful and above all as the 'Lord of all creation.'

Sometimes our worship lacks the sense of reverence, the sense of coming before the Almighty God, because we have lost the sense of transcendence. We become almost flippant in our worship. Yet what is unique in God's revelation of himself is that, unlike other religions that have a concept of transcendence (in Islam Allah is to be feared because of his greatness), our God also reveals himself in his immanence.

In Roman Catholic and Eastern Orthodox theology immanence is used to describe how God can be found anywhere in creation because he is active in all of it. In other words, he is not so far removed or above all that he cannot be known. But immanence needs to express something more than that. It needs to communicate that God can be known because God *desires* to come close to us. As the Psalmist writes: "Hear, O LORD, and answer me...." The Hebrew in this verse conveys the idea of "bowing to listen" (Ps. 86:1).

Psalm 113:6 asks: "Who is like the LORD our God, enthroned on high who stoops down to look...." Or, as the King James Version renders it: "humbles himself to behold." The Psalmist conveys both concepts of God—"above all," yet wanting to "come close" to us.

While all the names for God express something unique about him, it was his personal name or his covenant-making name that would express both concepts of transcendence and immanence.

God reveals his personal name in Exodus 3 when God talks to Moses through a burning bush. God gives Moses the commission, "I am sending you to Pharaoh to bring my people the Israelites out of Egypt." Moses responds with, "Who am I that I should go…?" In my paraphrase God replied, "It is not who *you* are. It is who *I* am."

Moses responds, "But what if your people challenge me and ask: 'What is his name?' What should I tell them?" God answers, "I AM WHO I AM. Tell them, I AM has sent me to you." The "I AM" God of your fathers – "the God of Abraham, the God of Isaac, and the God of Jacob—has sent me to you. This is my name forever, the name by which I am to be remembered from generation to generation" (3:14-15). He was saying to Moses, this is my covenant-making name, the name by which I have made my covenant with Abraham, Isaac and Jacob.

I AM (*YHWH*) as a name first of all expresses God's transcendence. It conveys the idea that God is not dependent on anything or anyone in creation. He is the self-sufficient One who is above creation.

I AM also expresses God's immanence. *YHWH* (Yahweh) as a name is from the verb "to be." But the verb in verse 12—"I will be (with you)"—is the same verb translated in verse 14 as "I AM" (*YHWH*). God reveals himself with the promise that he is our "God who is with us." He will be the God who comes close to us in whatever our situation may be. He is also guaranteeing that he will fulfill all that he promised. *YHWH* is not dependent on anyone else for his existence or for his ability to fulfill His promises. He is self-sufficient so that he can be the covenant-keeping God; the God who desires to be 'with us.'

Why is this important? Sometimes you may feel that your prayers bounce off the ceiling because you do not sense that God is there with you. Sometimes you feel that God is not close to you, not as you felt in the past. If so, then guess who moved? Not God. He wants to come close to you. He declares, "I will be with you." In Exodus 3 God says to Moses, "I am concerned about their suffering. So I have come down to rescue them."

The name "Jesus" reflects the same characteristic when the angel of the Lord said his name would be "Emmanuel—which means, 'God with us.'" When Jesus promised the Holy Spirit, the other Helper, Jesus used the word *paraclete* meaning the "one called alongside of." In each person of the Trinity we have the same concept of God wanting to be "with us" and to be close to us.

What an amazing picture for us! God wants to come close to us in whatever trial or struggle we are going through. He is the all-sufficient One for whatever I need, for whatever challenges I might be facing. The I AM God can be sufficient for me because he is self-sufficient.

Because God is with us then he also desires to be our JEHOVAH-JIREH: "The Lord will Provide"—to always be adequate for whatever need we face. He will be our JEHOVAH-ROPHE, "The Lord Who Heals" spiritually, physically and emotionally. The list of names continues with the same kind of reminders.

YHWH is all-powerful for whatever challenge we may be facing, but he is also our Abba Father who comes close to us and embraces us with his strong love.

Through His Covenant Love

When God shows relationship with his people he expresses his love in what I regard as the most powerful word in the Bible. It is the Hebrew word *hesed*. In almost every one of its 248 Old Testament occurrences *hesed* pictures the way that God loves us. It expresses his covenantal-love. In some translations *hesed* is rendered "unfailing love" (NIV) or "steadfast love" (RSV). The King James Version translates it "mercy" or "lovingkindness." As Nelsen's Expository Dictionary defines it, "*hesed* is not only a matter of obligation; it is also of generosity. It is not only a matter of loyalty, but also of mercy."[2]

The problem is that there are three intersecting concepts brought into this one word. It begins with the idea of love, but includes the concept of perseverance. Add to that the idea of strength, the ability to do what his love desires, and you have the meaning of *hesed*.

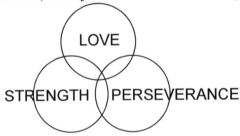

God continues to love us with a strong, persevering love even when we do not deserve it or are unfaithful in our love to him.

---

[2] Unger and White, p. 232.

How does this reality affect our spiritual vitality? We have all read accounts of a person suffering a tragedy such as paralysis, loss of limbs or facial disfigurement, while the spouse or fiancée continues to love despite the loss. How does the person receiving such love respond? With even greater love and appreciation because they know the usual human response is to leave.

In contrast to human love, God loves us with a strong, persevering love (*hesed*). As referred to earlier, Hosea provides us with a picture of this love. God tells him to marry Gomer, a prostitute so that Hosea would demonstrate strong, persevering love for her, the kind God shows to his people when they are unfaithful to him.

God makes this clear when he states his intent, "I will betroth you to me forever; Yes I will betroth you to me in righteousness and justice, in love (*hesed*) and compassion; I will betroth you in faithfulness, and you shall know the Lord" (Hos. 2:19,20).

That has been God's plan from the beginning. When we realize how he continues to love us in spite of our failures it should motivate us to a greater love for him. When we realize how he delights in a relationship with us, it should encourage us to enjoy our relationship with him even more.

Covenant love in the story of Ruth

The story of Ruth gives us another powerful picture of this kind of covenant-relationship. While the story of Hosea helps us identify ourselves as the unfaithful and undeserving recipients of God's covenant love, the story of Ruth illustrates the kind of love and commitment that God has shown to us in his covenant relationship.

Like a favorite movie that we enjoy seeing over and over again, let me push the 'play' button and put Ruth on the big screen of *His Story.*

The scene opens with an older Israelite woman, Naomi, walking with her two daughter-in-laws, Ruth and Orpah. They leave the city with their belongings on their backs. Naomi, her husband and two sons had moved from Bethlehem ten years before to Moab because of a famine. Their sons had married, life was good, and then tragedy struck. Both her sons and her husband died and she was left in this foreign land.

Hearing that the famine was over in Israel, Noami wanted to return taking Ruth and Orpah with her. As they began the journey, Noami realized that, as she needed to be with her relatives back home, they also needed to stay with their relatives in Moab. Noami loved both of them dearly, but she had no way of providing for them if they went with her. Naomi urged them, "Go back home. Go with my blessing. May *YHWH* (my covenant-keeping God) show you *hesed* as you have shown to your deceased husbands and to me."[3]

Orpah was persuaded and turned back. Ruth would not go back. Ruth exclaimed, "Don't urge me to leave you. Wherever you go I will go. Your people will be my people, and your God my God" (1:16).

Ruth was not only expressing her love for Naomi. She was also putting herself under the covenant of Naomi's God. As they arrived in Bethlehem the town buzzed with the news: "Naomi has returned, and she has brought with her Ruth the Moabitess."

Now the problem at hand was having food. So Ruth said, "Let me go to the fields and pick up leftover grain

---

[3] Ruth 1:7-9 (my paraphrase)

behind anyone who will show me kindness." "Go, my daughter," Naomi replied, and Ruth headed for a field hoping to find favor with the workers there (2:2-3).

In what appears to be a coincidence, she lands in the field belonging to Boaz. He is a relative of Naomi's husband and a "man of standing" in Bethlehem. Sometime during the day Boaz comes to the field to check on his workers. He sees this young woman hard at work.

"Who is she?" Boaz asks the foreman. "She is a foreigner, a Moabite, who just came back with Naomi from Moab. She asked if she could glean what had fallen among the sheaves. Boss, I couldn't turn her down. There is something about her. And she is some worker. In spite of the heat she just keeps going."[4]

Boaz approaches Ruth and tells her to continue working in his field with his servant girls. He promises his protection as well as provisions of water whenever she needs it. When she hears his concern for her and his urging her to stay in his fields she bows down with her face touching the ground. "Why have I found such favor in your eyes that you would even notice me—a foreigner?" (2:10)

Boaz tells her, "Everybody has been talking about you and all that you have done for your mother-in-law since your husband died, how you left your family and your people to live with us, a people you did not know. May *YHWH* repay you for what you have done. May *YHWH*, the God of Israel, under whose wings you have taken refuge, richly reward you" (2:12).

What Boaz was really saying was, "May our covenant-making God reward you for coming under his covenant."

---

[4] Ruth 2:4-7 (my paraphrase – continued through the narrative)

The next scene on the screen is mealtime with the workers and Ruth sitting next to Boaz. He offers her bread along with wine vinegar. The exchange is respectful, but somehow you feel the admiration Boaz has for Ruth, that it could build to be something of a love story.

When Ruth returns home to Naomi and recounts the events of the day, Ruth seems caught up in amazement at what has even happened. Naomi is pensive as she realizes this is more than coincidence. This is God stepping into their lives in an unusual way.

Naomi says to Ruth, "You know, there is a custom in our culture called 'kinsman-redeemer.' A kinsman-redeemer is one who is related by blood to the one he redeems. It is God's provision for his people if a husband dies and his land is held by another; or there are no children and his name needs to be preserved and given a heritage. We take care of it through a relative who becomes the kinsman-redeemer."

What Naomi told her was later described in Isaiah 59:17-21 and Deuteronomy 25:6 where a close relative has the responsibility to redeem family property that changed ownership. It also gives him the right to marry the childless widow when there was no brother.

Naomi then realizes that it is time for Ruth to test Boaz as to his willingness to be a kinsman-redeemer. Does his kindness show a great interest in, even desire for Ruth? What would he be willing to do?

Naomi instructs Ruth to put on her best clothes and best perfume. She is to go to Boaz in the evening when the harvesting is done. It sounds a bit aggressive to us today, but in her culture this action was proper and respectful.

Ruth follows Naomi's instructions. "When Boaz retires for the evening on his mat, go quietly to him and curl up at his feet under his blanket." Ruth did that while Boaz was sleeping but then in the middle of the night, he awoke when his feet hit something. It is Ruth.

Boaz asks, "Who are you and what are you doing here?" "I am Ruth," she whispers. "Give me covering since you are my kinsman-redeemer."

Kinsman-redeemer is the key word for Boaz. He admires Ruth. He even found his heart longing for her, but he never thought he could have her. He is older and less desirable than some of the younger men who could appeal to such a beautiful young woman. Now she has reminded him of his cultural obligation and even suggested that she is interested in him.

Before his heart can run away with that thought, he realizes that he cannot be her kinsman-redeemer. There is another relative who is closer and who has the right to redeem her first. Boaz is ready to put this man to the test as he formulates a plan.

As Ruth returns home and tells Naomi everything that has transpired, Naomi realizes that this story has passion and desire yet to be played out. "Wait, my daughter," Naomi tells her, "until you find out what happens. This man will not rest until the matter is settled today (3:18)."

Meanwhile (I love that word because it lets you know that more is happening to build this story), Boaz goes to the town gate where all business is transacted with the elders of the town. He waits for the man who has first right to be the kinsman-redeemer and confronts him. "You know that Naomi has returned from Moab and her property needs to be redeemed. You are the closest relative to do that. Tell me if you are willing to do it, because I am the next in line if you don't."

The man thinks, "I would like the land. I'll do it." When he says that, Boaz's heart sank. He takes a deep breath and replies, "Umm—did I mention that when you acquire the land you must also redeem the dead man's widow in order to maintain the name of the dead with his property? It is part of the deal."

The man realizes this is a complication he does not need. It endangers his own financial position, so he says to Boaz, "Buy it yourself." To seal the deal the man takes off his sandal and gives it to Boaz in front of the elders. It was a ritual that made the agreement binding.

Boaz's heart skips a beat as he tries to be calm and collected on the outside. On the inside he is bursting with excitement. He had acquired Ruth as his wife. The land is secondary. Love is what matters. This would be a love story pictured like no other—a marriage covenant formed by love, yet attained because of a kinsman-redeemer relationship.

The scene is now in the home of Naomi. Ruth is pregnant and the women say to Naomi, "Praise be to *YHWH* who has not left you without a kinsman-redeemer. May he [the baby] become famous and renew your life for your daughter-in-law loves you and is better to you than seven sons (4:14-15)."

As the music and picture on the screen lets you know that this story is coming to a close, we see Naomi holding a little baby. Boaz and Ruth have been married and have this little son, Obed (meaning "servant" or in its full form, "servant of *YHWH*"). Over the final scene the credits begin to roll – "Salmon the father of Boaz, Boaz the father of Obed, Obed the father of Jesse, and Jesse the father of David (4:22)."

This has now become the high point for the Jewish viewer – "Obed the father of Jesse, and Jesse the father of David." This is the line of King David, the line of the promised Messiah. Can any movie have a more exciting end than this?

Yet we realize this is our story as well. We are the foreigners to God's covenant of love. We are the ones in need of a kinsman-redeemer, and Christ becomes that for us. Through his coming close to us, God becomes our kinsman so that he could be our redeemer. In Christ we are brought under his covenant relationship so that he would claim us as *his people*.

Why is this such a powerful reminder? Because as foreigners we know we have no right to his love, yet he loves us anyway. When we come under his covenant we experience his strong, persevering love. As hard as it is to comprehend, the heart of God yearns for our fellowship, yearns for us to come running into his arms of love, and be embraced by our Redeemer.

Have you ever wondered what you could do to make God love you more? If you gave up all your possessions for those suffering in the Sudan or you went to some hard place in the world to serve him, would he love you more than he does now? The answer is: no. He already loves you to the fullest extent of his love. He merely invites you to respond to him in faithful love.

The purpose of his covenant-making is to remind us, as his people, of his commitment to relationship. When we understand what it means to be loved by a covenant-making God we will experience what it means to be part of God's story.

Study Questions:

1. There is a Christian song entitled, "Yahweh is for
    you." What does it mean to have a human friend
    who is for you? What makes it more significant to
    have "Yahweh for you"?

2. Read the story of Mephibosheth in 2 Sam 9:1-13.
    David says in verse 7, "I will show you loving-
    kindness *(ḥesed)*." In what ways are we like
    Mephibosheth (how does it describe our condition
    without God)? How is God's covenant relationship
    pictured in this account (how does it describe what
    God does for us)?

3. In Psalm 116:1 the psalmist exclaims "I love the
    LORD." It is with the passion of a teenager saying
    "I'm in love, I'm in love!" Read the psalm and note
    the outcomes or results in one's life of having this
    kind of relationship with Yahweh.

4. How does the story of Ruth speak to you as you
    think of God's covenant love?

5

HOW COVENANTS TELL THE STORY

"Tell us a story grandpa" – a common request when my grandchildren visit us. We all love a story.

Once there was a young man who always seemed to have everything going his way. When he was around the girls they whispered to each other how cute he was. They giggled at his jokes. He was fun and he enjoyed life. You could not help but like him. His father had achieved modest wealth and wanted to pass it along to his sons in a way that would help them be responsible adults. For his youngest son, responsibility was a stretch. This son was being pulled more and more into the values of a sinful lifestyle. There seemed to be nothing that the father could do to rescue him.

One day the son announced to his father that he was leaving home. He had possibilities of a career in another country. He had met a girl from there that he wanted to marry. He insisted that his father give him his part of his inheritance so that he could begin a new life for himself.

His father did not like what he was hearing, but his son was so insistent that he gave him what he wanted.

He tried to help him see how much wiser it would be to leave his money invested in the family business, but the son would hear nothing of it. He wanted it all, and he wanted it now.

So the son left for the dream of a new career and a new wife, but it was a fantasy. When he got to his new destination there was no job offer. There never was. The only work was day labor jobs and he was holding out for a management position. As for his girlfriend, she liked the party he could throw, but she was not ready for a serious relationship. With all the cute girls around, he was not either.

So life became a party—until the money ran out. Then the girls left. His friends left. He was hungry and there was no soup-kitchen to feed him. All he could do was get a job on a farm slopping pigs. He was so hungry that he would dip his hand into the pig food and fill his mouth just so he could stay alive. He never thought life could get this bad.

That is when he came to his senses. He realized that his father's employees lived better than this. He was so stupid to waste his life and his inheritance. Maybe he could have one more chance if he went back to his father, repented and begged for some job, such as sweeping floors or cleanings toilets. He hoped that his father would have a little bit of mercy for him when he saw how desperate he was.

What the son did not know was that day after day his father hoped for his son to return. His father paced the yard of his home looking out toward the road wishing for his son to come home.

As the son plodded towards home he rehearsed what he would say. He would tell him: "Dad, I have been so stupid. I wasted everything you gave me and I am so sorry. Can you ever forgive me? If you just make me like one of your employees I'll do whatever you want me to do." For the first time in his life he was saying something that he really meant. He was no longer trying to manipulate. It was too late for that. He knew he was in real need.

As he finally made his way up the road to the family home his father had already recognized him coming and was running toward him. The son tried to get out the words he had rehearsed along the way but he could not get them out. His father hugged him and kissed him. He put his expensive robe around his son's tattered rags. Every time the son tried to say something, the father kept interrupting with things like, "I am so happy to see you. Welcome home, son!"

Now, you know the rest of the story, because I just paraphrased an account that Jesus told in Luke 15. We all like stories. We particularly like this one because we know what he was saying was really about us. We were the prodigal son and our heavenly Father was the seeking father that longed for us to come home. Jesus wanted us to see with our emotions what it is to be loved by such a strong, persevering love when we did not deserve any of it. That is the essence of God's metanarrative of grace.

Jesus also told the story because it helps us see the big picture of God's plan of redemption and how he wants us to be part of his story. At this point it is helpful to step back and look at how covenants help us understand the metanarrative. We need to see the overarching covenant of grace in which God expresses his desires as the seeking Father. We also need to see the individual covenants as important chapters for telling the bigger story. It gives us perspective for seeing how God carries out his plan of redemption and restores relationship with us, his fallen creation.

However, one could respond, "But you don't need covenants to explain God's grace or his resolve to restore relationship." I would agree. You do not need to use the language of covenants to understand God's intentions and desires. Yet on the other hand, maybe we have missed something of significance by not understanding the purpose of covenants.

I would describe the importance of understanding covenant relationship by asking, "Do I need to wear a wedding ring to enjoy my marriage relationship?" The obvious answer is "no." My happiness in marriage is not dependent on that ring. However, the ring is an important reminder of a commitment that I made which directly affects my enjoyment of the marriage.

As with most couples, marital bliss has at times eluded us. I remember one occasion early in our marriage where we were so angry with each other that we threw our dinner into the face of each other. We have had our times of frustration and anger (much less with the passage of time) but we made an agreement early on that we would not use the "D word" – divorce. Whatever we were feeling, divorce was not an option. Such a commitment changes the way we deal with frustrations. It brings us back to our marriage covenant when we need it the most.

Renewing covenant commitment – his to us and us to him – helps us when we have our times of doubting. When we hear ourselves asking, "Does God still want to love me? Has he given up on me?" It is in those times that remembering commitments made and God's grace expressed that will get us through the hard stuff of life. To 'wear the ring' in terms of putting covenant relationship into practice is to remember the strength of commitment God has expressed to us. It should also give us courage to hold on to him.

The Covenant of Love

Covenants in Scripture are described in both general terms as the covenant of love and the everlasting covenant, as well as specific covenants God made with Israel or with Abram. When Daniel prayed: "O Lord, the great and awesome God, who keeps his covenant of love," Daniel was seeing God, in all of his covenant-making, as expressing his love. Even specific demands of the Law were an expression of his love and his desire for relationship with his people.

The following would be one way to paint the big picture so as to understand the overarching covenant that shapes his plan of redemption for mankind. It pictures God's creation in the beginning as being in right relation to God. That was the Garden of Eden. But with the Fall, God instituted a plan to bring mankind back into relationship, a plan centered in the cross, and culminating "at the renewal of all things, when the Son of Man sits on his glorious throne" (Matt 19:28).

God knows how to restore a fallen creation and to bring us into a right relationship with himself. The outcome is a covenant relationship; the process is covenant-making.

God's Plan of Redemption

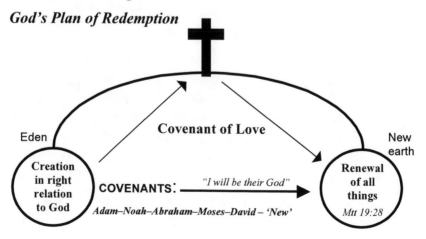

The Apostle Peter paints this kind of picture in Acts 3. He said, "But this is how God fulfilled what he foretold through all the prophets, saying his Christ would suffer." Peter is reminding the listener that before Christ came to earth the prophets foretold his coming, and that he would suffer, which the act of crucifixion inflicted on him.

When Jesus walked the Emmaus road with two of his followers after his resurrection he said the same thing: "Did not the Christ have to suffer these things and then enter his glory?" Then Luke records, "And beginning with Moses and all the Prophets, he explained to them what was said in all the Scriptures concerning himself" (Luke 24:27).

Jesus is the center point of Scripture and thus of all history. The Old Covenant leads us to the cross by making us aware of our moral need for an Intercessor. The New Covenant makes the Intercessor more personal (God with us) and leads us to his work of intercession through the cross.

In his Acts 3 message Peter points the listener to Jesus (v.16), calls for repentance (v.19), and says one must turn to him as Intercessor and Redeemer to experience the benefits of his covenant-relationship: (1) your sins will be wiped out; and (2) times of refreshing may come from the Lord (v.19).

Peter brings the end of the story into focus when he says, "He must remain in heaven until the time comes for God to restore everything" (v.21). This is the same promise of Matthew 19:28, "at the renewal of all things." This will be the final chapter of history, and Peter emphasizes again, that the prophets have foretold this long ago.

We have hope because God is in control of history and will one day fix the wrongs of this fallen world. In one sense, it is a fitting climax to a story so filled with pain. However, I think the real climax of Peter's message is, "You are heirs of the prophets and of the covenant that God made with your fathers. He said to Abraham, 'Through your offspring all peoples on earth will be blessed.'" (Acts 3:25,26)

Peter was reminding them that in the Abrahamic covenant ALL peoples will be blessed through his offspring—through the Messiah who came as Savior of the world. The story is not exclusive to the people of Israel but is a story of "every people, and tribe and tongue" (Rev. 7:9). It is a story that gives Israel, the nation promised from the seed of Abraham, a prominent role in accomplishing God's plan of redemption. It is a climax in which we can *all* celebrate. In fact, we will celebrate when Christ enters his glory.

In these few verses Peter gives the most concise summary of the plan of redemption to be found anywhere in Scripture. The picture begins with the promise pointing to Christ and concludes with a covenant that includes all peoples on earth. It reminds us that the cross of Christ is the center point of history. What the prophets anticipate we are able to fully appreciate when we too center our lives on the cross.

This is in essence the covenant of love which has been extended to every prodigal son. It is an act of God's grace that can be described through the language of covenant. While we do not need the language or terms to experience God's grace, the picture of covenant-making helps us better understand our need for a Redeemer in the setting of the big story. As we will now see, the individual covenants help us understand the unfolding of his plan that leads us to the Redeemer.

Adamic Covenant

This was not a formal covenant between God and Adam but an implied covenant because relationship was already established in creation. God created Adam in a right relationship and thus did not need what later covenants would do. As Adam walked with God in the cool of the evening he enjoyed a covenant relationship. The terms were to be faithful to God and to trust that God would provide for all of his needs.

The place of obedience was the two trees God planted in the Garden of Eden. Adam and Eve could enjoy everything in the garden including the tree of life, denoting God giving life without death, as long as they did not eat of the tree of knowledge of good and evil (Gen. 2:9-17).

Hosea 6:7 says that they were unfaithful to that covenant with God and in their disobedience sin entered the human race. From this point on, God uses covenants in the formal sense to lead man back to trusting God with complete devotion and faithfulness, a relationship intended from the beginning of creation.

Noahic Covenant

This is the first explicitly spoken covenant in the Bible. When we look at God's covenant-making and his covenant relationships, we will see how each major covenant in the Old Testament has a counterpoint or fulfillment in the New Testament.

After the fall of Adam and Eve, God pronounces a curse on creation (physical change of the serpent; thorns and thistles from the ground; soil needing hard labor) and on the human race (pain in childbearing; submission of wife to husband; work no longer enjoyable; physical death of mankind). The nature of man is also changed with a disposition towards sin. In fact, Genesis chapters 4 to 6 describe how quickly man becomes entangled in sin so that God grieves that he had made man. The text says, "his heart was filled with pain" so that he wanted to destroy mankind (Gen. 6:6).

"But Noah found favor in the eyes of the Lord." He was "righteous and he walked with God." Because of this, God preserved the human race through Noah and made a covenant with Noah. In this covenant God makes promises that will impact all creation and benefit all mankind. He makes a covenant to help man live in relationship with each other, as well as with God. The terms of this covenant are:

1) Animals are added to man's diet. The point of this was to demonstrate that man is responsible for managing all creation. God gave everything into man's hand to manage for his good, but also for the good of creation. The environment was a stewardship from God, to be used but not abused.

2) Man is responsible for orderly rule. The idea of government comes from God. God holds those in positions of authority responsible for fair and orderly rule. In Genesis 9:5 God says: "I will demand an accounting for the life of his fellow man. Whoever sheds the blood of man, by man shall his blood be shed, for in the image of God has God made man." This strengthens the sanctity of human life. It holds government responsible for protecting life. When evil men commit murder there is capital punishment. Paul writing to the Romans about those in civil authority said: "He is God's servant, an agent of wrath to bring punishment on the wrongdoer. Therefore it is necessary to submit to authorities..." (Rom. 13:4,5). If government does not do that, then God will hold its leaders accountable.

3) God promises to never destroy all earthly life with a
   flood. This is a promise of deferred judgment, and
   this is the most important point. Will God judge the
   earth again? Yes. There will be a final judgment of
   the earth and mankind that is described in the book
   of Revelation. One day God will say, "that is
   enough," and he will bring everything into
   accountability. Revelation chapters 20 and 21
   describe that final judgment and his creation of a
   new heaven and new earth. But until then, God
   promises to never bring this kind of judgment on all
   mankind. The rainbow is to be a sign of the
   promise that total destruction will not come again
   by water.

What is the value of this covenant? It helps me
value my relationship with God and my need for
submission to his rule. It also reminds me of social
responsibility to others in society and my
accountability to God for it.

Abrahamic Covenant

We have described God making his covenant with
Abraham earlier in this book. We find it recorded in
Genesis 12 and 15. The central feature is to "believe
God" (Gen. 15:6). The testing of Abraham's belief was
in the promise that they would have a son. Abraham
was 100 years old and his wife Sarah was 90 when the
promise was given. As a reminder of God's promise to
do the impossible, God changed his name from 'Abram'
to 'Abraham' meaning *father of a multitude.* So God
made a covenant stating (Gen. 12:2-3):

1) I will make you into a great nation
2) I will bless you
3) I will give you a land
4) I will make your name great
5) Through you all peoples on earth will be blessed.

As a sign of the covenant God requires circumcision of Abraham and his male offspring. As Youngblood explains:

> The operation is performed on the organ of reproduction because the covenant emphasized the procreation of descendants. The implication is clear: If the foreskin was not cut off, then the individual himself would be cut off from the people of God because the covenant would be broken (Gen. 17:14). The image is vivid indeed. Perhaps not so incidentally, the operation itself reminds us that covenants are solemnized only through the shedding of blood.[1]

Since the promise of the covenant was to make of him a great nation (Israel) and through his seed would come the One (Messiah) who fulfills the promise, "all peoples on earth will be blessed through you," the cutting of the male organ for giving his seed was an appropriate sign.

The covenant with Abraham is very significant because Christ would be the fulfillment of that promise and the scope of the promise is expressed in the Great Commission (Mtt. 28:19). As we take the gospel to all peoples of the earth we participate in the promise to Abraham, a promise which will receive its ultimate fulfillment in the final destiny of the redeemed. When people from "every tribe, people and language are standing before the throne and in front of the Lamb," the mission mandate of the Abrahamic covenant will be complete (Rev. 7:9).

What is the significance of the Abrahamic covenant for us? It reminds us of God's heart for all peoples and the extent he will go in calling them into relationship. It is a relationship of birthing a people to be used in

---

[1] Youngblood, *The Book of Genesis: An Introductory Commentary,* p. 170.

bringing forth the Messiah, the One who would provide the way to be in right relationship with God.

Mosaic Covenant

While there are references to God's covenant with Isaac and Jacob these seem to be affirmations of the covenant with Abraham. The next formal covenant that God cuts is with Moses and the people of Israel. The setting is Mount Sinai after God had called his people out of Egyptian bondage. His stated intent is that they would be a people holy to the Lord. The Mosaic covenant is detailed in Exodus 19-24, with the two main components being the Law and a pledge to be Israel's Protector.

In the Mosaic covenant, God sets forth his standard of righteousness so that man will realize his total inadequacy and his moral need for a Redeemer. This is called the Law in that it contained the Ten Commandments, as well as other regulations for living holy unto the Lord. What was the purpose of the Law? Paul says in Galatians 3:19, "It was added because of transgressions until the Seed to whom the promise referred had come." The Law was never intended to make one righteous but to show the righteousness of God and "to lead us to Christ that we might be justified by faith" (3:24).

The Law pictures this tension of holiness that was required for relationship with God and points to a Redeemer who restores relationship to God. The redemptive symbols in the tabernacle, the sacrificial system of burnt offerings and fellowship offerings, the schedule of feasts portraying the metanarrative of redemption—the feast of Unleavened Bread that began with Passover, the feast of Harvest (Weeks) that began with Pentecost, and the feast of Ingathering

(Booths) that will be fulfilled at the conclusion of history—all picture Christ in his work of redemption.

As a sign of the Mosaic covenant, the Sabbath as one of the commandments was given to represent the Law. "You must observe my Sabbaths. This will be a sign between me and you for the generations to come, so that you may know that I am the LORD who makes you holy" (Exodus 31:13).

Youngblood explains that the covenant with Moses was not a brand new relationship. Rather, it is best understood as...

> the logical outgrowth and expansion of his covenant with Abraham and his descendants six hundred years earlier (Gen. 15:9-21, 17:1-22). As the participation in the divine blessings of the Abrahamic covenant was conditioned on obedience and faith so also the Sinaitic covenant was conditional: "If you obey me fully and keep my covenant, then out of all nations you will be my treasured possession."[2]

What is the significance of the Moasic covenant to us today? First, it leads me to Christ. It shows me his standard of righteousness and my inadequacy to achieve that righteousness by my own efforts. It helps me realize how I need to desire holiness and how that holiness can only be found by being in Christ and by Christ working in me.

Davidic Covenant

God's covenant with David is found in 2 Samuel 7. God promises David that Israel will have a godly king; that this king would come through his seed; and that he would rule on the throne of David forever. In other words, it is an everlasting kingship that will only be fulfilled in the Messiah.

---

[2] Youngblood, *Everyman's Bible Commentary, EXODUS,* p. 92.

This covenant is appealed to by the descendants of David even though they did not do what was right in the eyes of the Lord. During the exile there is the hope of restoration under a Davidic king who will bring peace and justice.

The greatest significance of the Davidic covenant is that it points us to the Promised One (the Messiah). Psalm 2, which reflects on the covenant with David, is frequently quoted in the New Testament as applying to Christ (Greek word for Messiah), the great Son of David. Matthew begins his gospel with "the genealogy of Jesus Christ, the son of David, the son of Abraham" (Matt. 1:1).

The angel of the Lord announces to Joseph that "you are to give him the name Jesus (meaning '*YHWH* saves') because he will save his people from their sins" (Matt. 1:21).

What is the significance of the Davidic covenant for us today? It is important because it too brings us to Jesus, the center point of history. Following the lineage to Jesus we see the failures of David and the kings who would come after David. We realize the mercy of God in using such fallen instruments to display his glory. And in realizing God's mercy, we realize that God can use us too.

New Covenant

While all the previous covenants were mediated through a man (Abraham, Moses, David), the New Covenant was mediated through the God-man ("Christ is the mediator of a new covenant" Heb. 9:15). The other covenants lead us to Christ by helping us realize our need for Christ.

In the New Covenant, Christ leads us into a new relationship whereby he works in us through the Holy

Spirit. It is a personal relationship of *God with us* in the person of Christ.

The basis of both the Old and New Covenants was faith (i.e. faith in God) but the working of righteousness in the Old Covenant was an external one by man. It was helping the seeker realize his need for an intercessor.

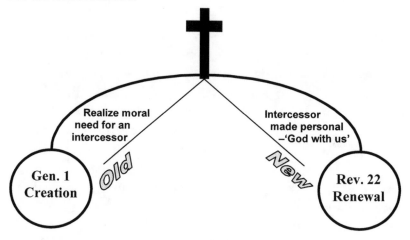

In the New Covenant, the Spirit's work is not just an anointing *on* the believer but a work *in* the believer. It is an internal re-creating by God.

The Intercessor is made personal by being made in the likeness of man (Phil. 2:7) so as to become the God-man. Jeremiah 31 looks forward in time and describes the New Covenant as:

1. **I will put my law in their minds and write it on (in) their hearts** (v.33). This is the work of the Holy Spirit who now resides in us as his temple. Jesus says the Counselor sent to you from the Father is the "Spirit of truth" who helps us do his will (Jo. 16:13).

2. **I will be their God and they will be my people** (v.33). The purpose of the covenant will be achieved, restored relationship with God.

**3. No longer will a man teach... 'Know the Lord':
for they shall all know me** (v.34). Personal
fellowship is a privilege of the New Covenant. We are
given intimacy with God whereby we can call him
"Abba Father" (Gal. 4:5). Jesus says: "I will not pray to
the Father for you, for the Father himself loves you"
(Jo. 16:27). This kind of intimacy was rarely found in
the Old Covenant but is now expected in the New.

**4. I will forgive them and will remember their
sins no more** (v.34). "For" begins this phrase in the
text and shows the reason for all that precedes it. All
this is possible because of the forgiveness through the
New Covenant. No other sacrifice for sin is required.
The sacrifice is so great and of such divine power that
it accomplishes all that is required by the holiness of
God. We remember our sins and live with our guilt,
but how does an omniscient God not remember? This
phrase reminds us that his forgiveness is so great and
final that he chooses not to remember our sins. As J.
Vernon McGee declared: "He puts them behind his
back and God doesn't turn around."[3]

Significance of the New Covenant

Realizing what is being offered to you and what the
gospel offers to others makes it the best possible news
anyone can have. That is why the Apostle Paul talks
about the ministry of the Spirit through the New
Covenant as being even more glorious than the
ministry of Moses (2 Cor. 3:7-8). Its significance is:

• *A covenant of grace*

No matter who you are, no matter what you have
done, God's grace is offered to you. It is on the basis of
his grace because the Old already proved that you
cannot conquer sin in your life, no matter how hard

---

[3] Quote from radio broadcast of Through the Bible by J. Vernon McGee.

you try. Like the Apostle Paul, be overwhelmed by his grace to you. Identify yourself as being "crucified with Christ" and living in him (Gal. 2:20).

• *An everlasting priesthood*

Under the Old Covenant only a select few (Aaron's priesthood) could enter the tabernacle. Under the New Covenant (Christ's priesthood) you are able to come into his presence with full assurance that God accepts you and desires to you "to draw near" (Heb. 10:19-23).

• *Ministers of the Spirit*

You are made "competent as ministers of a new covenant" (2 Cor. 3:6). Paul says, if you thought the old had glory, wait until you see the new. "Will not the ministry of the Spirit be even more glorious? ...the ministry that brings righteousness" (2 Cor. 3:8-9). Do you need motivation for being light in this world of darkness? Embrace the privilege of being ministers of this New Covenant, of declaring the best news the world could ever hear.

Climax of the Covenant

The culminating point for understanding God's plan of redemption is given to us in the individual covenant to Abraham. It forms the cornerstone of what God would do in history.

One finds the covenant climax in the promise that "all peoples of the earth will be blessed through you." This is the promise of the Messiah and what he offers through his New Covenant. William Dumbrell says, "The kingdom of God in global terms is the goal of the Abrahamic covenant."[4] Everything leads to this result and should inspire greater commitment to "all peoples of the earth."

The climax of the Abrahamic Covenant is the Great Commission: *Go and make disciples of all nations.* His mission becomes our mission—our "co-mission."

How many times do we hear God speak in the Old Testament of his concern for the nations? Psalms 67:7 reminds us that "God blesses us (so that) the ends of the earth will fear Him." Zechariah 2:11 says, "Many nations will be joined with the LORD in that day and will become my people." Or Zechariah 8:23, "In those days ten men from all languages and nations will take firm hold of one Jew... and say, 'Let us go with you because we have heard that God is with you.'"

The heart of God is to claim all peoples of the earth as "my people." Under the Old Covenant the mission was focused on one nation. Under the New Covenant the mission was to all nations. The good news is—God desires a covenant relationship with all who would say, "You are our God and we are your people."

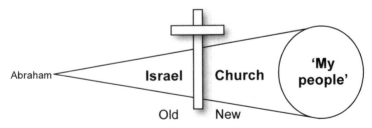

- Old Covenant – a mission for a nation
- New Covenant – a mission for all nations

---

[4] W. J. Dumbrell, *Covenant and Creation,* p. 78.

Study Questions:

1. Each of the individual covenants that comprise the Old Covenant seems to have a counterpart in the New Covenant. For example, the covenant with Abraham has its counterpart in the Great Commission, the covenant with Moses has its counterpart with the Spirit writing his law on our hearts. What would be the counterpart of the covenant with David and with Noah?

2. God's covenant is reiterated with Isaac and Jacob by attaching his name to theirs – "the God of Isaac, the God of Jacob." What would be the reason for doing this? Does God attach his name to ours? Reference Hebrews 2:11-13 and 11:16.

3. Read Exodus 20:1-17 (*Ten Commandments*).

    State a contemporary application for each commandment as to why it is important for society today.

4. In your own words, how did the individual covenants tell the 'big story' (metanarrative) of God's covenant-making? How is this reflected in Hebrews 11?

5. When you take part in the Lord's Supper and hold the cup that Jesus said was "the New Covenant in my blood," what should you think about related to covenant relationship?

6. How is the "sending of God" (Jo. 20:21), the *Missio Dei,*[5] reflected in God's covenant-making?

---

[5] *Missio Dei* is a Latin term for the "sending of God," the idea that God is the one who initiates and sustains mission and we join him in his mission.

6

OLD PICTURES OF THE NEW COVENANT

One day a mother was trying to explain to her little daughter that the picture she was holding of Jesus was not really a picture of Jesus. It was what an artist thought Jesus might looked like. The little child studied her picture a little longer and then replied, "But it sure looks like Jesus."

When we begin to understand the nature of our covenant relationship with God we will see how Christ is pictured in the covenants. Nothing more clearly represents that picture than the images of the Old Testament tabernacle. The images are not the work of an artist that we hang on a wall, but are pictures that will become clear as we walk through the tabernacle and see how see the Promised One is portrayed.

The tabernacle Moses made became the design for various temples to follow. These were not permanent, but they were never meant to be. They were the focal point of God's presence among his people under the Old Covenant. They also served a larger purpose of picturing the Anointed One who would come to fulfill the image of the tabernacle and its subsequent structure, the temple.

The temple built by Herod the Great was 15 stories high but the actual floor layout and dimensions of the Holy Place and Holy of Holies followed the former temples of Solomon and Zerubbabel. Herod began rebuilding in 10 BC. The outer courts were not completed until 64 AD and then the entire structure was demolished by the Roman general Titus in 70 AD.

When Jesus walked into the temple it was a new, polished structure of which the Jews were extremely proud. When Jesus said, "Destroy this temple and I will raise it again in three days," you can understand why they got so upset. The Jews replied: "It has taken 46 years to build this temple and you are going to raise it in three days?" But the temple he had spoken of was his body. (cf. John 2:20)

In the Jewish mind the temple structure was a permanent tabernacle. However, the writer of Hebrews says the sanctuary is just a copy and shadow of the tabernacle in heaven. It pictures something of greater glory. When we come to the book of Revelation, the final chapter in God's story, that tabernacle-temple is described for us. The apostle John writes in Revelation 21 that he sees the New Jerusalem. The beauty is breath taking. But then John looks for the temple and he cannot find it. Where is the temple? Verse 22 says: "I did not see a temple in the city, because the Lord God Almighty and the Lamb are its temple."

What he sees is the permanent temple. The tabernacle Israel carried around in its wanderings; the temples that Solomon and Zerubbabel built (Herod rebuilt) were just temporary pictures of the real thing— the Lamb of God. To make sure that we did not worship brick and mortar, the Bible tells us that we, who are part of the New Covenant, are the temple of God. God *presenced* himself in us, not in a physical structure. The Old and New Covenants both look forward to the day when we are in the presence of Christ and realize that is no temple there. Christ is our temple. None other is needed.

This structure called the tabernacle will describe some very important pictures of the Lamb of God, our Messiah Redeemer. With images of the Old Covenant it will picture a New Covenant relationship. Walk with me through the tabernacle, not as a tourist with all the historical facts, but as one worshiping the Messiah who is pictured for us in its symbolism. We need times of being renewed in our relationship to God. We need times of looking into the face of Jesus and desiring to see his glory. That can happen as we walk through the tabernacle.

The Tent of Meeting

From where we stand we see the tents of the people all around us. But this tent called the "tabernacle" was a special tent for meeting with God.

The priest moves into the courtyard surrounding this tent as worshipers bringing their sacrifices. The structure before them is the tent of meeting which has two rooms: the Holy Place and the Holy of Holies. Around the tent is a fence making the court area the place where the worshipers gather. It is about 7.5 feet high with only one door. You could not look over the top. You could not get in through any other way except the door.

This is a reminder that while God *presenced* himself in the middle of camp so that he was close to his people, they were separated from God and had to come to him on his terms. They could not make up their own religion, invent their own spirituality, or decide what is good enough for God. God would not be a holy God if he bent the rules or had different standards of holiness.

If, as Romans 3:23 says, "we all have sinned and come short of the glory of God," the question still facing us is: how can one approach a holy God? Is it even possible? Through the pictures of the tabernacle, God demonstrates how it is possible for someone unholy to approach a holy God. What we are about to encounter as we follow the priest will remind us that our God has made us for relationship with himself. Every image we will see shows how he has made a place for renewing our covenant commitment to him and enjoying relationship with him.

Altar of Burnt Offering

Before we enter the tent we approach an unusual looking altar where worshipers bring their sacrifices. The first man is offering a pigeon. The second is well dressed and has brought a young bull. Rich or poor, anyone can bring a sacrifice before God. The most common offering is a lamb. The reminder is that there is always a provision for the sin that separates us from God.

On this altar is where the sacrifice for sin is made. Exodus 38 describes it as a box made of acacia wood overlaid with bronze. It measures 4.5 feet high, 7.5 feet long and wide. It has a horn on each of its four corners.

In making the offering Leviticus 1:4 says, "He is to lay his hand on the head of the burnt offering and it will be accepted on his behalf to make atonement for sin." Sin had to be punished. It could not be ignored. It was an offense against a holy God with the penalty being death, ultimately physical and spiritual death.

The amazing part of the story is that as soon as sin entered the human race God provided a sacrifice for sin. After Adam and Eve sinned, God gave them the covering of an animal skin. There was an animal sacrificed to have a covering for their shame, which represented their sin. Under the Old Covenant the covering of sin was from the sacrifice made on the altar of burnt offering. The sin covering was not in the animal itself but how it pictured a greater sacrifice for sin that was to come. God was fulfilling vicarious sacrifice: God accepting one's sacrifice on behalf of another for the covenant relationship to be renewed.

Without a sacrifice the problem everyone would face would be, how could one die for one's own sin? But if someone who was without sin could die in another's place, then the penalty of sin would be removed. The worshiper brings a lamb without any defect to be sacrificed. No bone was to be broken, because it would be the picture of the Lamb of God who would be sacrificed for the sins of the world.

John 19:37 quoting Zechariah 12:10 "they will look on me, the one they have pierced" makes sense for worshipers at the crucifixion of Jesus when they would realize that it pictures Jesus as that lamb who was pierced for our sin. He became the perfect sacrifice who was without sin, yet took on himself our sin. He was struck, "smitten by God the Father." He took on himself what should have been the punishment laid on us.

As the worshiper brings his sacrifice, the priest puts the lamb on the bronze altar and then with the worshiper's hand on the head of the sacrifice the priest cuts the throat of the animal. The priest catches the blood of the sacrifice in a bowl and sprinkles the blood on the sides of the altar. Once a year on the Day of Atonement the high priest takes the blood of the altar and sprinkles it before the veil as he enters the Holy of Holies, then on the seat of the ark itself. It is a reminder that the only way we approach a holy God is on the basis of the sacrifice made for our sin.

When Christ instituted the New Covenant through his own sacrifice, he showed how he would be God's sacrificial lamb and how our covenant relationship with a holy God could be renewed (cf. Heb. 9:11-15).

In his death he provides atonement once and for all. The old image leads us to the new reality where God forgives our sins and "remembers them no more" (Jer. 31:32). When I, so to speak, lay my hand on the cross of Christ, I take his sacrifice as mine. He forgives my sin and releases me from the guilt that I carry.

Why is this important picture for us today? When my conscience reminds me of my sins and my inability to approach a holy God, I ask, "Is there anything that can cleanse me?" The answer comes back: there is nothing that can, nothing but the blood of Jesus.

Laver

The worshiper lingers in the courtyard and we watch the priest as he goes to the laver, a bronze basin that stood between the altar of burnt offering and the tent of meeting. There the priest washes himself before entering into the tabernacle.

How is the laver an important covenant picture? The laver serves as a reminder of the daily need for cleansing. In the Old Covenant water and blood are both symbols of how God provides cleansing for us as we come before him in our worship. On the altar of burnt offering blood was spilled and the substitute for our sin was paid, but the laver was the reminder of our need for maintaining fellowship with God.

Obedience was expected. Disobedience "broke the covenant," meaning the relationship, in the same way that disobedience breaks or hinders the relationship of parent and child. In the evangelical tradition of worship we do well at celebrating the forgiveness of *sin*—the sin question that separates us from God—but sometimes we need the reminder of the importance of confession of *sins*. We need cleansing of sins in our daily walk. We pick up the dust of the street on our hands and our feet, where we go and what we do. We need to be washed of those things that hinder our fellowship with God.

In the New Covenant we are instructed, not to go to a physical laver, but to go to Jesus seeking his cleansing. 1 John 1:9 promises us, "If we confess our sins, he is faithful and just and will forgive us our sins and purify us (cleanse us) from all unrighteousness."

He promises to wash away our sins if we come to him wanting his cleansing. Our problem is that we often excuse the little sins in our life rather than confessing them.

Having lived in Ethiopia and Bolivia, I have experienced both parasites and amoebas. At first you can ignore it, but after a while you start feeling drained of physical energy. Then you start feeling sick. The best advice is to not ignore it; deal with it.

The same advice holds for spiritual things. When the Holy Spirit convicts of the little sins in our life, do not ignore it or excuse it. Deal with it. Confess it. Come to 'the laver' for cleansing so that it does not drain away your spiritual vitality and become like a cancer in you.

Zechariah 13:1 pictures the Messiah as "a fountain ...to cleanse from sin and impurity." Christ deals with both the sin that separates us and the sins that hinder relationship. His commitment is to "forgive us our sins and cleanse us from *all* unrighteousness."

Lampstand

We now follow the priest as he enters the Tent of Meeting. There is a lampstand to the south side. It is made of pure gold and has six branches with cups shaped like almond flowers to hold the oil and wicks of the lamps. He checks to see if the lamps need trimming or the cups need oil. The flames are flickering to give light to the Holy Place.

In the tabernacle and in the temple of Zechariah's time there was one lampstand. In Solomon's temple there were ten. Whether tabernacle or temple, the lampstand was a reminder that "God is light and in him there is no darkness at all" (1 Jo. 1:5).

Jesus made the personal application of this to himself when he said: "I am the light of the world" (Jo. 8:12). If he is the light then we as his followers are to be his lightbearers.

In the Old Covenant we find the idea of God's people as lightbearers. In Zechariah 4 God uses the lampstand to picture his people being lightbearers to the other nations around them so that they would come under his covenant. The purpose was so that "many nations will be joined to the Lord in that day and will become my people."

This is an important message because it tells us what it means to be his covenant people. That term will include not only those from the Jewish nation but from every nation and tongue who are joined to the Lord. It means we will be a people on a mission to carry his light to the dark places of the world: places where people live in fear of evil spirits, where AIDS is destroying lives, where children are sold into slavery, where idolatry reigns and people have no saving knowledge of Christ.

Now the natural response would be: but how can we ever do that? We do not have the ability or strength for such a task. But then Zechariah 4:6 reminds us, it is "not by might nor by power, but by my Spirit." God provides something greater. "You shall receive power when the Holy Spirit comes upon you and you shall be my witnesses...to the ends of the earth" (Acts 1:8).

The lampstand pictures how God uses us to carry his light. Under the Old Covenant the mission was *centripetal* (going towards the center). Israel was to show God to the nations around them so the non-Jew would look to the Jew and say, "Let us go with you (to worship) because we have heard that God is with you" (Zech. 8:23).

Under the New Covenant the mission is *centrifugal* (going out from the center). The Great Commission expresses it with Jesus saying, "Go and make disciples of all nations..." We are to be lightbearers for the One who is the Light. We are to be sent ones on a mission to go out to the nations.

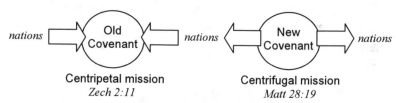

Centripetal mission
Zech 2:11

Centrifugal mission
Matt 28:19

The Apostle Paul wrote to the Corinthians that with this mission "we are Christ's ambassadors, as though God were making his appeal through us" (2 Cor. 5:20). God's plan for calling the nations to a covenant relationship is through us. We are to be his light, but in Isaiah 42:6 the Lord intensifies the mission: "I will keep you and will make you to be a covenant for the people and a light for the Gentiles."

How is the lampstand an important picture of the New Covenant? It is a reminder of being missional.

Having a sense of mission and being caught up in God's mission in our world is at the heart of what it means to have a covenant relationship with God. The New Covenant as prophesied through Jeremiah gave the mandate of declaring good news going to all nations. The Abrahamic covenant put focus on this being fulfilled in the Promised One. As the priest nurtures the flickering lampstand there is a reminder of a much greater story to come.

When that story comes to its close, John writes in Revelation 21:22, "The city did not need the sun to shine on it for the glory of God gives it light and the Lamb is its lamp. The nations will walk by its light." Until then we are to be his lightbearers declaring the Light of the world.

Table of Bread

With the lampstand burning brightly the priest now turns to the north side of the Holy Place and approaches the table of bread (or showbread). The table was made of acacia wood overlaid with pure gold. The plates and dishes were also made of pure gold. The Lord instructed: "Put the bread of the Presence on this table to be before me at all times" (Ex 25:30).

There were 12 loaves of bread which represented the 12 tribes of Israel. This being a Sabbath the priest sets out new bread on the table and takes the old loaves out for the priests to eat. This was to be a picture of God providing for our needs. "This bread is to be set out before the Lord regularly, Sabbath after Sabbath, on behalf of the Israelites, as a lasting covenant" (Lev. 24:8).

In Buddhist temples of Asia food is set out to feed the gods. In their minds, the people are taking care of their god. Zechariah 10 begins with the reminder that it is the Lord who takes care of us, who "gives the showers of rain and plants of the field." We are to look to him for our daily needs. We are to learn a dependence on God in our daily life. Jesus reminded us of that in the Lord's Prayer – "Give us this day our daily bread" (Mtt. 6:11). He would be the one who provides for our physical and spiritual needs.

In our self-sufficiency we forget that Jesus provides for us, until disaster hits. When we get the bad report from the doctor; when we lose our job and can no longer provide for our daily needs; then we cry out to God. But we have it all wrong. Dependency on God is to be our pattern of living, our first response.

The bread of the Presence was a daily reminder of his covenant promise to be with us and to provide for us. It is also a reminder that we need to come to him each day hungry for his righteousness; hungry to know God more as we walk through our day.

Jesus gives us this model in the Lord's Prayer because we need to be reminded of the pattern of dependency and the attitude of seeking after God. One of the ways you can refresh that in your own heart would be to stop reading and take a moment of quietness to slowly pray the Lord's Prayer (Matt. 6:9-13). As Henri Nouwen says, to see "the caring face of our compassionate God."[1]

In that prayer you will experience the one who said, "I am the bread of life." You will find him to be the one who fulfills all that is pictured at the table of the Presence. He provides for us in our physical life. He provides in the protection of our spiritual life. As we desire physical bread we also need to desire him. He is to be the passion of our life, the longing of our heart.

---

[1] Henri Nouwen, *The Way of the Heart,* p. 90.

Altar of Incense

The priest then approaches the third piece of furniture in the Holy Place which is the altar of incense. This is made of pure gold and stands before the veil that separates the Holy Place from the Holy of Holies. On it the priest offers special incense that is made of three spices. It is to be unique from any other fragrance and not duplicated for any other use.

Offering incense on the altar was the closest anyone would get to the presence of God. In the Bible, the idea of incense ascending is a picture of our prayers ascending to God. Psalm 141:2 says: "May my prayer be set before you like incense."

Revelation 8:4 pictures the opening of the seventh seal where all of heaven stands in silence for about half an hour. Then one of the angels takes a golden censer and at the altar offers incense together with the prayers of the saints. The smoke of the incense rises up before God and before his throne.

That is how God pictures our prayers. He views it as incense rising to his throne room—whether it is our praise or our problems. He delights in hearing it all. Sometimes we forget what a privilege it is to have God care for us that way. In Zechariah 12:10 the Lord says, "I pour out...a spirit of grace and supplication" (a seeking for grace). God wants us to have a spirit of seeking his grace—seeking God for all of life.

From my years in Ethiopia I was humbled by the commitment of some of my brothers and sisters there to prayer. Dick McClellan who served as an SIM missionary during the Communist period (the Derg) had some amazing accounts of God answering prayer during those years of persecution. He said on one occasion he was speaking at a church conference in a remote area when they recognized the dust clouds of the approaching army vehicles. Knowing that it meant trouble, a group of women dove into a hut just as the vehicles circled the gathering of believers.

The army captain in charge was drunk and began to taunt Dick as the foreigner leading the group. At one point he became so angry that he commanded his subordinate to shoot Dick. The soldier pushed the barrel of his rifle into Dick's chest and pulled the trigger. But his finger froze.

He pulled his hand away and shook it, and then tried again. But his finger froze. At this point the captain in great anger grabbed the rifle and shoved it into Dick's chest, but when he pulled the trigger his finger froze. In frustration he threw the rifle to the ground and jumped into his jeep to drive off. When he came he was not driving, but when he left he was at the wheel and sped off in a cloud of dust.

A short distance away he lost control on a curve, hit a large rock and was killed. The women who took cover in the hut were not running away. They were the prayer group for the conference. They were the ones to take this desperate situation to the throne of God.

I recognize that God does not always answer the way that we want. Sometimes the loved one dies or the cancer is not healed. Sometimes we lose the house or our job. Paul says, we may be "hard pressed on every side but not crushed" (2 Cor. 4:8). In every situation, God steps into our lives in unusual ways with peace and provision when we turn to him in prayer.

The altar of incense reminds us that our prayers are not a nuisance to God but rather ascend to him like a sweet smelling savor. In the same way that I delight in the smell of fresh baked bread, God delights with the fragrant aroma of our prayers which ascend to the very throne of God.

Ark of the Covenant

In our walk through the tabernacle we now encounter a picture of God's overwhelming majesty and holiness. We pass through a heavy curtain into a small room (15 by 15 feet) with one box like piece of furniture. The room is called the Holy of Holies. The piece of furniture is called the ark of the covenant. The mystery of this room is in the picture of God's holiness and how we commune with a holy God.

The tabernacle has two rooms: the Holy Place which is the focal point of daily communion by the priests, and the Holy of Holies which the high priest enters once a year on the Day of Atonement. On that day he represents himself and the whole nation of Israel in seeking atonement or a covering for their sins.

The prescribed ceremony for the priest is to take blood from the altar of burnt offering and sprinkle it on the altar of incense. After this he sprinkles it before the veil that opened the way into the Holy of Holies. Then he takes the altar of incense with him into the Holy of Holies. The smoke fills the room with darkness. In that sense it hides the priest from God's holiness. That is why the hymnist wrote:

> Holy, holy, holy! Though the darkness hide Thee,
> Though the eye of sinful man Thy glory may not see;

It was in the darkness of smoke from the incense that the glory of God came to the Holy of Holies. Man could not look on God's glory because of his sinfulness. Yet God provided a way for man to come close to God. The priest would take the blood from the altar of burnt offering and sprinkle it on the seat of the ark of the covenant. In that act there was a covering for man's sin and a sense of coming close to God.

What was unique about the ark of the covenant for this moment? It was a box made of acacia wood overlaid with pure gold. Its dimensions were three and three-quarters feet long by two and one-quarter feet wide and high. The atonement cover was made of pure gold with two cherubim out of hammered gold at the ends of the cover. "The cherubim had their wings spread upward, overshadowing the cover with them. The cherubim faced each other looking toward the cover" (Ex. 37:9).

Cherubim are first mentioned in Genesis 3:24 where immediately after the fall they are guarding the Garden of Eden and the tree of life. In the tabernacle their image is woven into the curtain and sculptured into the ark of the covenant. In Ezekiel 10 and several references in the Psalms cherubim are described as belonging to the throne of God and intimately connected to the presence of God.[2] So the image of the cherubim represents the guardians of the God's glory, not to prevent man from experiencing his glory, but to keep man from the consequences of entering into God's presence in man's sinful condition.

Inside the ark of the covenant are three things: a pot of manna representing God's provision for his people; Aaron's rod that budded representing God's rule or authority over his people; and the two tablets of the Law representing the standard of God's holiness. When the priest stood before the ark which symbolized the throne of God, he represented a nation of sinners needing atonement so they could meet with God. In Exodus the Lord says, "There above the cover between the two cherubim that are over the ark of Testimony I will meet with you..." (Ex. 25:22).

---

[2] W.G. Moorehead, *Studies in the Mosaic Institutions*, p. 77.

That meeting took place at the mercy seat. Moorehead says, "It is spoken of in the Scriptures not simply as the lid or covering of the ark, but as a distinct object, almost as if it did not belong to the ark (Ex. 30:6, 31:7, 35:12)."[3] It symbolized a judgment seat based on God's standard of holiness and picturing the throne of God's glory. When the blood of the sin offering was sprinkled on the covering, it became a mercy seat. God showed his mercy, not by giving us what our sin deserved, but by giving us what we did not deserve—his grace. Atonement was complete.

Why is this Old Covenant picture so significant to us who are now under the New Covenant? It helps us understand what took place at the crucifixion of Christ. He died in darkness as his death completed the atonement for our sin. It was an awesome moment that represented both the holiness of God and the laying on Christ all the punishment that our sins deserved (Is. 53:4-5). His blood had to be sprinkled for my sin for me to experience God's mercy.

Is it be possible to fully understand the significance of being under the New Covenant if we did not have the Old Covenant picture? We who are part of the New Covenant are in danger of becoming so accustomed to his grace that we fail to live in awe of his great mercy.

This picture of atonement in Old Covenant gives us a better picture of Christ and the great grace and amazing love he has shown. It is a picture that brings us before the throne of God not in fear but with confidence because of Christ. It is what the writer of Hebrews was able to see:

> Since we have confidence to enter the Most Holy Place by the blood of Jesus, by a new and living way opened for us through the curtain, that is, his body,

---

[3] Ibid., 80.

and since we have a great priest over the house of God, let us draw near to God with a sincere heart in full assurance of faith, having our hearts sprinkled to cleanse us from a guilty conscience and having our bodies washed with pure water. (Heb. 10:19-22)

We, as people of the New Covenant, should be overwhelmed with a sense of God's holiness and then bow before our God, not in the rituals of worship but with a heart of worship.

To understand that truth is to understand the New Covenant in which we exclaim:

Holy, holy, holy, though the darkness hide Thee,
Though the eye of sinful man Thy glory may not see;
Only Thou art holy, there is none beside Thee,
Perfect in power, in love and purity.

God is revealed in the pictures of the tabernacle to be awesome in his holiness and his glory. Yet he is revealed as the God who comes close. If we did not have the Old Covenant and the images of the tabernacle could we have understood this? Could we have seen Jesus in all his glory?

The benediction of Hebrews 13:20 seems to reflect the importance of covenant pictures in realizing the full story of redemption, "May the God of peace, who through the blood of the eternal covenant... through Jesus Christ, be glory for ever and ever. Amen."

Study Questions:

1. Read Hebrews 9.

   How does each article of the tabernacle build toward the climax of the ark of the covenant?

2. The ark of the covenant contained 3 items:
   a. Gold jar of manna
   b. Aron's staff that had budded
   c. The tablets of stone of the covenant

   What do you think was the significance of each for the Israelite of that day? What does each of these items say for us today?

3. Today we do not have physical articles of the tabernacle to give us important reminders of our worship. How can we accomplish the same thing in worship without the physical articles?

   Suggested small group activity:
   "Walk through the tabernacle" reviewing the meaning of each article or piece of furniture and conclude each section by singing a song that expresses the meaning of that article (e.g. Altar of Burnt Offering – sing "Nothing But the Blood of Jesus," or other appropriate song)

7

MAKING THE PROMISES STICKY

The word "sticky" has become the new term for making the Christian faith transformational. We have books with such titles as *Sticky Faith*, *Sticky Church*, *Sticky Teams*. The idea is that people come in and out of a church without making their faith stick; without personal transformation because the church has failed to find meaningful application of God's truth. A sticky church for example uses a small groups ministry to help one find connection and commitment.[1] A sticky faith is one that brings real change—one that sticks through times of testing.

C.S. Lewis once said, "Some Christians have just enough truth to inoculate them against its effects." In other words, the desired result of applying God's truth is transformed lives. But if we only take it in small enough doses to make us feel good, without letting it become sticky, then the result is spiritual anemia.

The reason God allows or even brings into our lives difficult times is so that we can experience his truths having its desired effect.

---

[1] *Sticky Church* and *Sticky Teams*, both books authored by Larry Osborne and published by Zondervan.

When facing trials that seem overbearing, D. L. Moody used to say, "Run to the promises!"[2] When your world is falling apart and you are desperate for something to lean on, run to the promises that God has given you and hold on to them. God wants his promises to be sticky in your life.

What does this have to do with covenants? I see God's covenant-making as his way of saying, "This is more than a promise that you flippantly speak. This is a commitment that you can hold on to; it is sticky because of who I am."

Old Testament Promises

Habakkuk the Old Testament prophet complained that evil men succeed and God does nothing. You can almost hear the prophet pleading, "Why do you let them get away with murder? Do something." God answers him, "Wait."

"For the revelation awaits an appointed time; it speaks of the end and will not prove false. Though it linger, wait for it; it will certainly come and will not delay" (Hab. 2:3).

God assured Habakkuk that he has not forgotten his people nor his promises. God tells him that he sees those who "piles up stolen goods," those "debtors who suddenly arise and make us tremble," those who are unjust and criminal in what they do (Hab. 2:6-7).

I can identify with Habakkuk when I remember how I and two others were taken to court over a homeowner's association issue. Those were days of intense stress. When we presented our case to the

---

[2] D.L. Moody quoting Samuel Rutherford: "In your temptations, run to the promises: they may be our Lord's branches hanging over the water that our Lord's silly, half-drowned children may take a grip of them," *Letters of Samuel Rutherford* (Oliphant Anderson & Ferrier, 1891), p. 107.

judge giving irrefutable proof that the other side had perjured themselves and falsified financial records, the judge ruled without even reading our papers. I was feeling the whole situation was unjust and criminal. I wanted God to zap the bad guys, or at least make sure that they did not win. Habakkuk's situation was worse. It was life and death. God still said 'wait.'

Waiting is so hard. Yet it is in waiting that God changes us. We learn what it means to trust the God who makes promises through his covenants. It is in waiting that we give time for God to act.

Waiting also gives time to shift our focus from ourselves to God. The Lord concludes his words to Habakkuk with the reminder of focus: "But the Lord is in his holy temple, let all the earth be silent before him" (Hab. 2:20).

Waiting, being silent, gives time for trusting God with our difficult circumstances, but also for reminding ourselves that God is in control of all the messes and stresses of life. His promises remind us that he is still in control. When he brings history to a close, the earth will be silent before him. The wrongs will be made right. Knowing that we can learn a quiet submission right now; waiting for him to do what is best and what will bring him the greatest glory.

Challenging Our Idolatry

Israel continually struggled with idolatry in spite of God's faithfulness to his people. In the Lord's word to Habakkuk he says: "Of what value is an idol, since a man has carved it? Or an image that teaches lies? For he who makes it trusts in his own creation; he makes idols that cannot speak... Can it give guidance? It is covered with gold and silver; there is no breath in it" (Hab. 2:18, 19).

Having idols seems incredibly stupid. Why would anyone worship something created with human hands and then value that more than the God who created the entire universe? As I reflected on the stresses of my life in these past years, I found myself confronted with the same issues. I had to own up to a certain kind of idolatry in my life that God was allowing to be exposed through crisis.

The mess and distress of my life began when my wife and I decided to conclude our missionary service and I took a position with a Christian university. The president enthusiastically supported what I was doing but my immediate boss did not. I knew as soon as the president retired, which was coming soon, my boss would terminate my position. My safety net would always be, "Talk to the president. He will tell you how I did." The only problem was, the president died of a heart attack nine months after he retired.

Then to add to the stress, not long after that my mother died and left us with a terrible financial mess. We faced the threat of losing our home and everything that I counted on for retirement. In those dark days of fretting I found myself pleading with the Lord, struggling with how to get out of such a mess.

What the Lord was saying to me through it all was, "You need to confront the idolatry in your life." Of course, I would argue, "How could I be accused of idolatry? I have been a pastor, a mission's leader, a seminary professor. Idolatry belongs to the heathen or ancient Israel, but not me."

I was listening to a message by Tim Keller on Colossians 3:1 in which he talked about idolatry as taking the good and making it the ultimate—making it the most important thing in our lives. He asked:

- "What things in your life if you were to lose them would make you feel you didn't have a life left?"
- "What things do you turn to in order to go on?" [3]

I was convicted that my idolatry was taking a good thing (my service to the president) and making it the ultimate thing in my life (the thing that determined my value and worth). When I was in my pit of despair I would try to jest by saying, "I'm looking for a bridge to jump off." It seemed from my vantage point that I had no future.

By taking a good thing—my vocation, my home—and making them the ultimate thing, I had made them my idols. God allowed me to go through this time of waiting as a time of cleansing. If Christ was the ultimate thing in my life, if I had truly set my affections on Christ, then why did I slip into such despair? It was simple. Idolatry had crept into my life.

His Promises Today

The process of struggling and waiting can be exactly what we need. It can be a time of purifying and a time of learning to run to the promises. In saying that, we also need to be careful that the promises we claim extend to us, and are not specific to Israel for that time and situation.

For example, the promise of: "None of your women will be childless nor any of your livestock without young. The Lord will keep you free from every disease." (Deut.7:14-15) These were specific to Israel entering the Promised Land and not a blanket promise for all time. In fact, in other biblical accounts there are examples of the people of God being barren and getting sick.

---

[3] Tim Keller sermon: Christ our Life, Sept 18, 2005.

In looking at the promises of God, Mark Strauss would emphasize the hermeneutic of differentiating a promise made *to* us versus a promise being *for* us (for us to learn from it). Jeremiah 29:11 is often quoted as a promise to "prosper you and not to harm you, plans to give you hope and a future." Was that *to* us or *for* us? The promise was to the exiles in Babylon. The message in context was that they would be in bondage for 70 years, after which the Lord says, "I will fulfill my gracious promise." Are we willing to accept that his good may come to us through extended hardship? That was part of the promise.

We like to sing, "The Lord has promised good to me, his word my hope secures." At first it sounds like we think the promise is that nothing bad will happen to us. Whereas if his good for us is the product of him "working all things for our good" (Rom. 8:28), then it does bring a different perspective to my trials. I may have to go *through* them believing God will work them together for my good.

Having said that, what are his promises that God's people in all times can hold on to? Here are a few:

Psalm 29:11 – "The Lord gives strength to his people."

Psalm 32:8 – "I will instruct you and teach you in the way you should go."

Psalm 34:4 – "I sought the Lord and he answered me; he delivered me from all my fears."

Psalm 34:18 – "The Lord is close to the broken-hearted and saves those who are crushed in spirit."

Psalm 84:11 – "No good thing does he withhold from those whose walk is blameless."

Romans 8:28 – "God works all things together for the good of those who love him."

James 4:8, 10 – "Come near to God and he will come
near to you...Humble yourselves before the Lord and
he will lift you up."

1 Peter 5:7 – "Cast all your anxiety on him because
he cares for you."

Many are the promises in Scripture that are given
to us, that can be claimed by us. Most of all, we have
the assurance, "The Lord is faithful to all his promises
and loving toward all he has made" (Ps. 145:13).

Does this mean that God always rides to the rescue,
puts down the bad guy, and delivers us from all our
trouble? Habakkuk expresses confidence that the Lord
will act in his time against the invading nation. He
says, "I will wait patiently," but then he ends with:

Though the fig tree does not bud and there are no
grapes on the vines, though the olive crop fails and
the fields produce no food, though there are no sheep
in the pen and no cattle in the stalls, yet I will
rejoice in the LORD, I will be joyful in God my Savior.
(Hab. 3:17,18)

Habakkuk has just described the worst of economic
times, the times when we would feel most desperate,
and yet he is able to say, "I will rejoice in the LORD."
How could he say that? It was because God was
ultimate in his life.

My wife's wisdom on this is, "Sometimes we read
Scripture so focused on finding what God is saying to
us *(e.g. through his promises),* that we miss how God is
revealing himself in this passage—his character, his
actions. If we come wanting to know God, we will find
him."

God promises to teach us, to satisfy us, to make us
glad (cf. Psalm 90, 103). For Habakkuk to experience
his "rejoicing" it meant his first desire had to be
'knowing God.' It is a matter of focus.

Priority of Hearing

When my priority is to know God and his character then I will be ready to hear what he wants to say to me. If my focus is hearing words that I want to hear, then I may misinterpret Scripture meant *for* me and read it as *to* me.

In my past couple years, when my life almost ended through a car accident or my financial security seemed threatened, I wanted to hear promises such as, "I set before you today life and prosperity" (Deut. 30:15). I wanted to hear, "Beloved, I pray that you may prosper in all things and be in health" (3 Jo. 2 NKJV).

Can I pray for health? Can I pray to prosper in what I do? Yes, I have confidence in asking because of my covenant relationship with God. Jesus said, "How much more will your Father in heaven give good gifts to those who ask him" (Matt. 7:11). But if my first concern is focused on knowing God who demonstrates faithfulness and commitment, then it will affect what I ask for and how I read his promises.

Like Habakkuk his promises may lead me into valleys that I do not want or call for commitment from me that is not easy. Yet his promises always remind me that he is a covenant-keeping God and he always speaks, "I will be with you."

Remembering the Covenant

Israel had a way of forgetting the covenant and their commitment to the Lord. They would forget that with his promise to provide for them, the Lord also said, "Walk in obedience to all that the Lord your God has commanded you" (Deut. 5:33). Because of this the Lord required renewal of the covenant through periodic reading of the covenants.

Youngblood states the covenant documents "were to be read aloud to the people of Israel assembled in holy convocation once every seven years (Deut. 31:10-13) as frequent reminders of the responsibilities to which the tribes had voluntarily committed themselves."[4]

In 2 Kings 22 and 23 we have a covenant renewal ceremony. This is possibly the last example of such a renewal before the destruction of Jerusalem and the exile of Judah in 586 BC.[5]

The act of remembering did not keep Israel from sinning, but it was an important step in renewing their commitment to the Lord. We have the same need today as Israel had then. We easily forget out commitments and we need to renew our declaration, *You will be our God and we will be your people.*

As people of the New Covenant we are told to remember and renew our commitments when we take part in the Lord's Table. As Youngblood notes:

> The first communion meal shared by Jesus and his disciples inaugurated a new series of covenant renewal ceremonies as proclaimed in Christ's own words of institution: "This cup is the new covenant in my blood. Do this, as often as you drink it, in remembrance of me." (1 Cor. 11:25)[6]

Unfortunately in many of our evangelical churches the communion celebration is a five minute addendum tacked on to the service. There is little contemplation and reflection that allows for renewal of commitment. In our haste to complete the ritual might we be missing an opportunity to make the faith 'sticky'? Could we be inoculating believers against the effect of

---

[4] Youngblood, *The Heart of the Old Testament,* p. 52.

[5] Ibid, p. 54.

[6] Ibid. p. 56.

their declared faith—keeping them from a lived-out faith?

In Israel's covenant relationship with God the nation would be given signs of their particular covenant which served as a reminder of their commitment. For them it was possible that the sign lapsed into a postscript with little thought of what the sign meant.

Is it possible that the sign did invoke a renewal of commitment to the covenant? Did Noah and his family pause whenever a rainstorm gave way to the beauty of a rainbow and remember God's promises? Did Abraham and his descendants have cause to remember every time a son was born and on the eighth day the rite of circumcision was performed? Did the family fuss over the blood that was spilled or did they celebrate that this was a son of promise, a child of the covenant?

After Israel was given the Mosaic covenant with the Law and its sign of the Sabbath celebration, did each Sabbath give opportunity to remember and renew their commitment, or did the people lapse into ritual and forget the purpose of their seventh day rest? When on their Sabbath celebration they read from the Scriptures that they had, if the reading delineated a genealogy, did it cause a pause of reflection on the promise of a Messiah-king who would be born in this line of David?

For the faithful, each event could have been a moment of remembering and renewing their covenant relationship. And remembering was not confined to the sign-celebrations. Joshua erecting a monument of stones, Israel collecting of manna during the dessert wanderings or celebrating the Passover each year, all gave opportunity to rehearse and renew. There was also the encouragement for private moments of parents with their children. "Teach them to your children, talking about them when you sit at home and when you walk along the road..." (Deut. 11:19).

Remembering and renewing is also important for us today. As people of the New Covenant with the sign-celebration being the cup and bread of the Lord's Table, could this be our opportunity for renewing our commitment to God or teaching our children to make a commitment of their own?

The promises of God become *sticky* (bring change to our life) when we "make God the ultimate," more than make our desires the ultimate.

Sometimes the promises lead us through difficult times. Laura Story penned her song, "Blessings," when her husband was diagnosed with a brain tumor. She prayed, "Why didn't you just fix it God? You're all powerful and all loving. Just fix it." After expressing her longing to return to normal, her sister replied, "Maybe the detour is actually the road."

Laura realized that "spending time with Martin (her husband) obviously makes me happy, but it makes me a better person. That's the blessing of it." In the lyrics of her song she wrote:

What if your blessings comes through raindrops,
What if your healing comes through tears,
What if a thousand sleepless nights
Are what it takes to know you're near.[7]

In the desperate moments of life, "run to the promises." Let them lead you to a covenant-keeping God who desires to come close to us, who brings you to what Habakkuk experienced: "I will rejoice in God, my Savior."

---

[7] Song by Laura Story, BLESSINGS (New Spring Publishing).

Study Questions:

1. Read Hebrews 8

    Every time Israel celebrated a feast or a Sabbath there was the reminder to "love the Lord your God and serve him with all your heart" (Deut. 6:4). In the New Covenant what are the reminders for his people given by the writer of Hebrews?

2. How do you decide which promises of God was written *for* you and which were written *to* you?

3. Reflect on the Laura Story song, *Blessings,* and ask: How does one make the promises of God "sticky"?

    > We pray for healing, for prosperity
    > We pray for Your mighty hand to ease our suffering
    > All the while, You hear each spoken need
    > Yet love us way too much to give us lesser things.
    >
    > 'Cause what if Your blessings come through raindrops
    > What if Your healing comes through tears
    > What if a thousand sleepless nights
    > Are what it takes to know You're near
    > What if trials of this life are Your mercies in disguise.

Suggested: Consider celebrating communion at home or with your small group so as to discuss the meaning of communion. Celebrate it with praises and prayers for renewing commitment.

8

How Theology Looks at Covenant

When you mix theology with covenants, the first question to be asked: Is this about covenant theology?

How you view the topic of covenants will be different depending on your theological lens (Reformed, Lutheran, Baptist, Anabaptist, Arminian). My purpose is not to present a theological position. In fact, I have resisted talking about theologies because I felt it was more important to discover what the Bible has to say about covenants and covenant relationship before we try to defend our place in a theological system.

I do not wish to minimize the importance of a theological position, but I also do not want to make it the central focus of this book. My concern is to reawaken us to a vital truth about our relationship with God, that is, God brings us into a sacred bond of commitment through covenant-making in which God commits himself to us and we commit ourselves to God.

Our theological lens influences our perspective of covenants, so we need at least a brief overview of theologies. My greater desire though is to deepen our relationship with God by understanding covenants.

Theological Implications

Covenant theology and dispensationalism are two theological traditions that have made covenant the central motif of their doctrinal systems. While most evangelicals today do not align themselves squarely within either of these camps, most have been significantly influenced by these two frameworks.

For example, the differences between the two will show themselves in views about Israel and the church: does the church replace Israel in terms of the promises God made through his covenants? Is the church a parenthesis in God's plan or an expansion of God's plan? Does covenant within the God-head become the influencing factor of describing predestination—the decree of electing by God over the decree of allowing free will by man? Does a covenant relationship of the parents have any implications for the children of this covenant household? If so, does baptism become a symbol of the New Covenant in the same way that circumcision became a symbol of the Old Covenant? What about the interpretation of end times? Is the millennium literal or figurative? Is the second coming of Christ a single event or in two stages? What is the meaning of the Lord's Supper—do we receive grace by Christ being spiritually present in the elements or do we just memorialize grace given through the sacrifice of Christ? These are but some of the issues affected by our theology of covenants.

J. I. Packer, a Reformed Anglican, argues that a consistent reading of Scripture leads one to a true knowledge of God and his way of working with sinners. "Once Christians have gone this far, the covenant theology of Scriptures is something that they can hardly miss."[1]

---

[1] J.I. Packer, *Introduction to Covenant Theology,* p. 3.

Berkhof and Covenant Theology

Covenant theology, also called Reformed theology, has been articulated by several notable biblical scholars. Louis Berkhof (1873–1957) was a Reformed theologian best known for his *Systematic Theology* (1932) in which he laid out the structure of covenant theology. Berkhof followed in the line of John Calvin and embraced the development of Reformed theology by Dutch theologians Abraham Kuyper and Herman Bavinck. In that framework covenants became the organizing paradigm for the biblical text.

Meredith Kline (1922-2007), R.C. Sproul or Michael Horton would be referenced as today's spokespersons for covenant theology.

Some claim that concepts foundational to covenant theology can be found in the writings of the church fathers such as Irenaeus and Augustine. Church historian, Scott Clark, traces the use of covenant through the middle ages. He writes:

> ...the word "covenant" became synonymous with "law." They did not speak of a covenant of works and a covenant of grace, as we do. Rather the grace of the covenant enables one to keep the law.[2]

Clark states that Martin Luther differed from this interpretation because he viewed all of Scripture as having two ways of speaking: law and gospel. The law demands perfect obedience, and the gospel announces Christ's perfect obedience to that law, his death and his resurrection for his people.

Caspar Olevianus (1536–1587) followed Luther and taught the covenant of grace is made only with the

---

[2] R. Scott Clark. Ligonier Ministries website, Tabletalk article, *The History of Covenant Theology,* Oct 1, 2006.

elect. The elect are united to Christ by grace alone, through faith alone, in Christ alone.

Covenant theology views the big picture of God's dealings with mankind in all of history from the framework of three overarching theological covenants: the covenants of redemption, of works, and of grace.

These three covenants are called theological because they are not explicitly presented as such in the Bible but are implied through the various descriptions in Scripture. Proponents of covenant theology present it as a covenant of works that extends from the creation of man to the Fall, and a covenant of grace implemented from the Fall until the consummation of history.

Covenant of Redemption

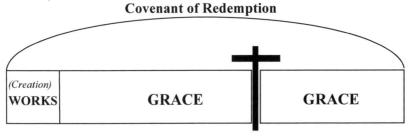

| (Creation) WORKS | GRACE | GRACE |

The nature of God's covenantal relationship with his creation is not considered automatic or that God is required to implement such a plan. Rather, God voluntarily established relationship through a covenant, wherein the terms of the relationship are set down by God alone according to his own will.

In particular, covenant theology teaches that God established two covenants with mankind, flowing from one eternal covenant within the Trinity called the covenant of redemption.

The covenant of redemption is the eternal agreement within the Godhead in which the Father appointed the Son by the power of the Spirit to redeem the elect from the guilt and power of sin. Because of the eternal covenant, God-the-Son was to be incarnate in human flesh, live in perfect obedience to the law, and then die a substitutionary, sacrificial death as the covenantal representative for all who trust in him.

The covenant of works was made between God and Adam in the Garden of Eden. It promised life for obedience and death for disobedience. Adam, and all mankind represented in Adam, broke the covenant, thus standing condemned before God. The covenant of works continues to function after the Fall as the moral law.

Though not explicitly called a covenant in Genesis, the comparison of the representative headship of Christ and Adam in Romans 5 and the reference of Hosea 6:7—"like Adam they have broken the covenant"—has been interpreted to support the idea. Jeremiah 33:20-26 (cf. 31:35-36) compares the covenant with David to God's covenant with the day and night, and the statutes of heaven and earth that God laid down at creation.

The covenant of works can be seen as the moral law component of the broader creational covenant. It is the natural law in the human heart.

The covenant of grace promises eternal blessing for all people who trust in the successive promises of God. Christ is the ultimate fulfillment of these promises. He is the substitutionary covenantal representative fulfilling the covenant of works on their behalf, in both the positive requirements of righteousness and its negative penal consequences through his obedience to the will of God. It is the expression of God's plan in history of the eternal covenant of redemption. Genesis 3:15 promises the "seed" of the woman would crush the serpent's head. This is usually identified as the historical inauguration for the covenant of grace. This larger covenant becomes the basis for all future covenants that God makes with mankind.

The individual covenants with Noah, Abraham, Moses, and David are called the biblical covenants because they are explicitly described in the Bible. Under these covenants, submission to God's rule and living in accordance with his moral law (to be expressed in the Ten Commandments) is a response to God's grace. It can never be something which earns God's forgiveness or acceptance.

Covenant theology makes some distinction between the Old and New Testament periods, but views it as one covenant of grace which was "differently administered in the time of the law and in the time of the gospel." They are of one substance "under various dispensations."[3]

Scofield and Dispensationalism

John Darby in the early 1800's articulated the theological system of dispensationalism. It was further developed by Cyrus I. Scofield with the publishing of the Scofield Reference Bible in 1909.

The term dispensation is used to translate the Greek word *oikonomia* (1 Cor. 9:17; Eph. 1:10; 3:2,9; Col 1:25). According to Charles Hodge, principal of Princeton Theological Seminary (1851-1878) and defender of Calvanism, dispensation means a plan or scheme when used in respect to one in authority. When used for one under authority, it means a stewardship or administration as in the management of a household.

In Ephesians 3:9 Paul writes that God kept as a mystery this plan (*oikonomia*) of his grace being

---

[3] Berkof, p. 278.

extended to the Gentiles. God's covenanted plan of redemption is one of grace, but that grace is revealed in two dispensations: the Old Covenant (Mosaic dispensation) and the New Covenant (Christian dispensation).

If we ask how a person is declared righteous in the Old Testament, the answer would be, "by faith." Paul makes that clear in Romans 4 where he is quoting Genesis 15:6 and also 22: "Abraham believed God and it was credited to him as righteousness." Paul continues in 4:13, "It was not through the law that Abraham and his offspring received the promise that he would be heir of the world, but through the righteousness that comes by faith." Verse 16 indicates, "The promise comes by faith so that it may be by grace and be guaranteed to all Abraham's offspring."

God's plan has always been to redeem us "by grace through faith." In that sense, God's metanarrative has always been about showing his grace as the means to bring us into his redemptive plan. However, his grace was revealed and enacted in various schemes that act out his overall purpose.

Using Isaiah 32, Darby concluded that Israel, in a future dispensation, would enjoy earthly blessings that were different from the heavenly blessings experienced by the church. This meant that there was a clear distinction between Israel and the church. Darby's flow of events began with a rapture of all believers followed by Daniel's Seventieth Week (a seven year period of tribulation) in which Israel would once again take center stage in God's plan. After this, Darby believed that Christ would return to earth with all his raptured saints, and rule a literal millennial kingdom in which God would fulfill his unconditional promises with Israel.

Scofield outlined seven dispensations: Innocence (creation to the Fall), Conscience (Adam to Noah), Civil Government (Noahic covenant to Abraham), Promise (Abrahamic covenant to Moses), Law (Mosaic covenant to Christ), Grace (Pentecost to second coming), Kingdom (millennial reign of Christ). The tribulation period is added between Grace and Kingdom, but is not counted as a dispensation.

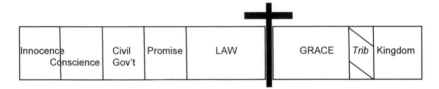

According to Scofield, a dispensation is "a period of time during which man is tested in respect of obedience to some *specific* revelation of the will of God."[4] In this system, covenants describe the testing man faces in order to show that he believes God and is faithful to the revelation that God has provided.

Under the Mosaic or old dispensation, the gospel was revealed in types and shadows. The Epistle to the Hebrews demonstrates this relationship between the old and new dispensations. The writer points to the tabernacle with its altar and mercy seat as a picture of what Christ did in providing atonement for us through the cross. As those under the Old Covenant looked to the form, they were to see a function beyond the symbol. It was an offering of the heart and not merely the requirement of the symbol. "Circumcise your hearts...so that you may love him with all your hearts" (Deut. 30:6); "Sacrifice and offering you did not desire...I desire to do your will" (Ps 40:6-8); "To obey is better than sacrifice" (1 Sam 15:22).

---

[4] Scofield Reference Bible, p. 5.

The writer of Hebrews then says, "They serve at a sanctuary that is a copy and shadow of what is in heaven" (Heb. 8:5) or what is to come. The writer goes on to describe how Christ has fulfilled those symbols and is seated in heaven, having completed his work of atonement.

Showing the transition from the old to the new the writer continues in Hebrews 10:8 "Sacrifices and offerings, burnt offerings and sin offerings you did not desire, nor were you pleased with them" (although the law required them to be made). Then he said, "Here I am, I have come to do your will." He sets aside the first covenant to establish the second. And by that "will" Jesus makes us holy through his sacrifice which was once for all.

Dispensational theology emphasizes that faith in the provisions of God's grace is required in the various dispensations. It is through the progressive revelation of his grace and the testing of obedience in each dispensation that gives man the opportunity to express faith in God's grace. In each the worshiper realizes that he is not able to meet the demands of a holy God and must rely on God's grace to be forgiven and accepted.

In this way the saving work of God goes beyond the symbol and the act of completing the ritual to the ultimate fulfillment in Christ. For the Old Covenant worshiper, it is still a mystery yet to be revealed but understood in the present in terms of faith and obedience to what has been revealed.

Differences between the two theologies

Dispensationalism seems to put more emphasis on the individual covenants as they progressively reveal God's plan of redemption while Covenant theology seems to put more emphasis on the over-arching covenant that pictures God's plan of redemption.

The two theologies have many differences that I will leave for individual study. The view of each regarding covenant relationship has affected their understanding of Israel and the Church, last things and the millennium, ordinances or sacraments of the church (covenantal signs and seals which include the Lord's Supper and baptism). The purpose of this discussion is to focus on the building blocks of the "big story" (metanarrative) and to understand how covenant becomes an essential element in God's plan of redemption.

I chose these two theological frameworks because in my view they have been the polarizing positions within the evangelical church. As previously noted, many evangelicals have difficulty being labeled by either position. Some have wondered: can there be a middle ground between the two theologies?

There are some dispensationalists who articulate a position called "Progressive Dispensationalism." This refers to the progressive relationship of successive dispensations to one another in which covenants are progressively fulfilled today and the present age of grace becomes a vital link in God's overall plan of redemption.

Traditional dispensationalists see the church as a parenthesis in God's plan in which Israel and the church are distinct "peoples of God" while progressives see Israel and the church as having two salvation-historical embodiments of the one "people of God."[5] As to the future of Israel, traditionalists see God's plans for Israel from the previous dispensation as being "put on hold" until it resumes again after the rapture.

---

[5] Pocket Dictionary of Theological Terms, p.40.

Progressives see more continuity between Israel and the church. They see both are related to the blessings of the New Covenant but they do not equate the church as Israel in this age. They see a future distinct identity and function for ethnic Israel in the coming millennial kingdom.

There is also another theological framework called "New Covenant Theology." This position typically does not hold to a covenant of works or one overarching covenant of grace. The essential difference is their view that the Mosaic Law as a whole is superseded in Christ and is no longer binding on the believer.[6]

How do you develop your own position? Read the arguments for each. Re-read Scripture describing these positions with the prayer that the Holy Spirit would help you understand what you need. Lastly, recognize that there are differences and there will still be differences when you are finished.

Though the list of authors could be more extensive my recommendation would be: for Covenant theology read works by R.C. Sproul, Meredith Kline or Michael Horton; for Dispensational theology read works by John Walvoord, Charles Ryrie or Dwight Pentecost; for Progressives read Craig Blaising and Darrell Bock or Robert Saucy.

Value of the Big Story

After struggling with these differing theologies, what is the value of looking at covenants and talking about the metanarrative—the big story? The most important value is that it helps us realize that the story is not about us but about God. We know that intellectually, but we continue to live as if it is all about us: my reputation, my resources, my goals.

---

[6] Desiring God blog, John Piper. January 23, 2006.

Seeing the bigger picture gives orientation to our goals and plans. It calls us to be Christ-centered.

Do I need that? Yes, I really do. I am the type of person who looks back over my life and reflects on all the mistakes or all the things I could done have better. If only life had 'do-overs'—what we delusional golfers call 'mulligans'—then we could do it right the second time around. The reality is, however we don't have do-overs. We have one life to live, therefore we need to live whatever the Lord gives us as an offering to him. Whether it is a few years or many years, with little recognition of others or fame, it is all his.

Seeing the bigger picture also reminds me that God is in control of history. I forget that at times. I think God needs me to worry about the mess of this world as if that is going to make it better. God does not like the mess either, but he knows when it is going to come to an end. When he closes the final chapter he will "restore all things" to his original plan and design.

Stepping back and seeing God's grace woven through history, whether from the dispensational perspective or from the covenant theology perspective, reminds me there is a bigger story, an overarching story of commitment and purpose.

Why should I care about the individual covenants? The most important reason is because they assure me of God's faithfulness. To me it all seems like a puzzle. To God it is a picture that fits together. Corrie Ten Boom at the end of the Billy Graham movie on her life, *Hiding Place,* sat talking with a tapestry on her lap. She showed how we see the underside with all the knots and mess of threads. In heaven we see the other side, the complete pattern in all its beauty.

I previously referred to the importance of the Hebrew word *ḥesed* in understanding of God's love.

Linked with the word *ḥesed* is often the word *emûnâh* –
'faithfulness.' The strength of God's unfailing love is
underscored in Scripture by the writers pairing *ḥesed*
with   *emeth*   ('truth,   reliability')   and   *emûnâh*
('faithfulness').

Why study covenant relationship? It is because we
all need the reminders of God's love and faithfulness.

When God demonstrates his unfailing love he does
it with concrete, specific acts that demonstrate his
promise. I need that reminder when there are clouds of
uncertainty on my horizon. They may cloud my
perspective but not God's. He knows where he is going
in history and his promises and reminders of covenant
relationship give me the hope that I need. In the words
of the song by Steven Curtis Chapman:

> In every situation
> He has proved his love for me
> When I lack the understanding
> He gives more grace to me
>
> My Redeemer is faithful and true
> Everything he has said he will do
> Every day his mercies are new
> My Redeemer is faithful and true.

Study Questions:

1. Read Jeremiah 31:23-40 and list the important features described in a covenant relationship with God. How are these features highlighted in either dispensational theology or covenant theology?

2. What are some of the wrong attitudes or views about Israel today that are reflected in either theology? Can you think of Scriptures to help answer your concerns?

3. What is the purpose of baptism (support with Scripture)? Look at both dispensational theology and covenant theology to see who better accomplishes that purpose.

4. What could either theology contribute to your celebration of the Lord's Supper?

9

MAKING IT PERSONAL

Ron Youngblood was an unpretentious scholar. He knew so much yet he was humble in how he dispensed that knowledge. His desire was to encourage people to "get into the Book." His primary concern was not persuading you to a theological position but inspiring you to more deeply know God and his Word.

Days before he died Ron recorded from his hospital bed his testimony. Ron told about a turning point in his life, how as a teenager he attended a Bible conference to hear one of his favorite preachers at that time. His name was Donald Grey Barnhouse, pastor of the Tenth Presbyterian Church in Philadelphia. That night Barnhouse challenged his audience to be fully committed to Christ and after the meeting, Ron talked with Barnhouse.

As Ron related Barnhouse's final words to him, Ron became choked with emotion. Barnhouse simply said to Ron, "Then get into the book." Ron said, "I paid careful attention to that. It began a life time of intensive Bible study for me." That set him on a path of desiring to know God even more and to be a devoted student of his Word.[1]

Ron told me that one of his favorite themes in Scripture was that of covenants and covenant relationship. If I could pass on my favorite theme of Scripture, it would be the same. As I think about the various projects of my life I feel more passionate about this project than anything else. My desire was not to produce an academic treatise on covenants but an invitation and motivation to explore what it means to have a covenant relationship with God. I honestly believe that in the exploring this truth we will receive something of that hidden treasure to which Andrew Murray referred.

The theme of covenant relationship is more personal to me because most of my Christian life and background has neglected this truth. I have known all the parts and pieces, but the concept of God's covenant-making has given it strength and made it cohesive. It has reminded me of how much God values me and wants to come close to me. It has helped me in my worship to both see God in his transcendence and his immanence—to be in awe of his majesty and yet to know he delights in my whisper of "Abba Father."

If this project has helped you find a deeper relationship with God or encouraged you to "get into the book" then it is worth the effort. Living with spiritual mediocrity is missing God's best for our lives.

Andrew Murray said "nothing will help us more in our work of intercession than the entrance for ourselves personally into what it means that we have a covenant God." By now the reader will have understood why he could make such a claim, but maybe two reminders are important. The concept of

---

[1] June 27, 2014 from his hospital bed.

covenant relationship reminds us that we can make our claim on God, but he can also make his claim on us.

Our Claim on God

Entering into God's covenant-making means that we can now lay our claim on God. His covenant is giving us a way to lay hold of God and all his resources for our life. There will be times when we feel all alone but we are not alone. *YHWH* is the one who says: "Do not be afraid for I am with you." He is the God who comes close, who is with us in all our struggles, in all our decisions of life.

I have said that the only reason I am in ministry today is because I had a professor who valued me and invested his life in me. When I was struggling with my sense of inferiority, Bill Bynum was there for me. He believed in me when I could not believe in myself.

The God of the Bible is that kind of Father to you, and more. Think of it. The God who made the universe is on your side. *YHWH* is for you! And your covenant relationship with him gives you a way to lay your claim on God, to bring before him whatever is the burden of your heart, and he hears you. He believes in you even if you can't believe in yourself. (cf. Ps. 139:14)

He invites us to lay our claim on God. Psalm 62:8 says, "Trust in him at all times, O people; pour out your hearts to him, for God is our refuge." In Psalm 89:24 the Lord assures us that "My faithful love will be with him, my covenant with him will never fail (v.28), I will not take my love from him" (v.33). Or Psalm 138:6 adds, "Though the Lord is on high he looks upon the lowly." Verse 8 then assures me, "The Lord will fulfill his purpose for me." The Creator-God in all his transcendent glory looks upon me with purpose so that

I can make my claim, "do not abandon the work of your hands."

Therefore, we can lay our claim on God. We are under his New Covenant. He has promised to be "with us," to "be our strength," to "care for us," to love us with an enduring, unfailing love. When life seems to overwhelm us and we do not know what to do, as his people we can ask him to remember his covenant. We can lay our claim on God.

God's Claim on us

But entering into His covenant also means that God can lay his claim on you. He can say, "I have redeemed you so that you would live with me in faithful love." He can say, "I want all of you." That is his right.

Sometimes we set boundaries or compartmentalize our life with God. We say to him, "You can have everything that relates to church or the spiritual stuff." God wants to lay claim on every area of our life —our recreation, our goals, our loves, our vocation. It is not only, "He is our God" but it is also our declaration that "we are his people."

1 Peter 3:15 says: "In your hearts set apart Christ as Lord." To lay hold of his covenant relationship is to declare him Lord of all. He may ask for our financial resources, or our health, or our plans. He may ask for anything that he can use to bring glory to himself. That is his right as our covenant-making God.

I may want to be healed, but he may say, "I can show my glory through you by not healing you." Or, "I can show my love to more people through you by using your weakness." If he is Lord, then he can ask to be Lord of all. He can ask us to put his glory on display through our sickness.

Ron Youngblood in his final recording echoed this when he said: "Whatever time I have left, pray that I would use it for his glory."

The glory of the New Covenant

In writing 2 Corinthians the Apostle Paul gives us personal disclosure of his struggles as well as the significance that he places on being part of the New Covenant. Paul begins by talking about "the God of all comfort who comforts us in all our troubles" (1:3). We are shocked when we read Paul's words, "we despaired even of life" (1:8). How could Paul be so distressed that he would say that? He continues, "But all this happened that we might not rely on ourselves but on God." God uses the hard stuff with purpose in our life.

Paul uses imagery of covenant-making when he says that God "anointed us, set his seal of ownership on us, and put his Spirit in our hearts..." (1:21-22) to make us stand firm in Christ. He uses language of the Old Covenant of not having our lives be on "tablets of stone" (3:3), but be a "letter from Christ" written by the Spirit of God.

His reminder is that when we are feeling our incompetence and lack of abilities we stake our claim that our competence is "not in ourselves, but our competence comes from God" (3:5).

> He has made us competent as ministers of the new covenant – not of the letter but of the Spirit; for the letter kills but the Spirit gives life. (2 Cor. 3:6)

Paul then describes being "ministers of the New Covenant" as being more glorious than what Moses experienced. While Moses may have veiled his face because of the external glory from God's presence, we have a greater glory—that of "reflecting the Lord's glory, being transformed into his likeness with ever-increasing glory" (3:18). It is an internal glory of reflecting Christ through our lives.

Is there any doubt as to the importance that Paul places on the privilege of being "ministers of the new covenant" and having this "ministry of reconciliation" (5:18)? Paul uses Old Covenant images of the temple with New Covenant significance saying, "we are the temple of the living God" (6:16). He invokes the covenant formula as applying to us as part of the New, "I will be there God and they will be my people" (6:16). Paul draws on the words of the Davidic covenant to remind us of God's immanence—his desire to come close to us—"I will be a Father to you and you will be my sons and daughters" (6:18).

When Paul reaches his most personal and intimate confession of 2 Corinthians 12 we sense the inner struggle of pleading with the Lord over his "thorn in the flesh, a messenger of Satan, to torment me" (12:7).

I think it was an eye disease that made him despicable to some (see Gal. 4:14). Paul says, "If you could have done so you would have torn out your eyes and given them to me" (4:15), which could have been a proverbial expression or it could be an expression that applied to a real situation. Paul writes at the conclusion of Galatians, "See what large letters I use as I write to you in my own hand" (Gal 6:11).

The point is that Paul found strength in the most difficult places of life by coming back to what it means to be in relationship with a covenant-making God. Hearing God say, "My grace is sufficient—my power is made perfect—my glory is made known" and to know that these were not empty promises, is only possible when we grasp the commitment of God through his covenant-making.

Paul not only knew hardships and distress to a greater intensity than I have ever known, but Paul also knew God and his unfailing love to a greater depth than I ever will know.

My personal story

It may be time to tell my story—one that for all of my life I have resisted relating. But I will tell it now because I think it will help you understand why this theme of covenant relationship is so important to me. What I struggled with mostly during my growing years was an eye deformity that caused a feeling of inferiority and lack of self-worth. You see, I was born extremely cross-eyed. Not slightly cross-eyed, but both eyes turning radically in.

For the first four years of my life we lived in northern Saskatchewan. Dad was a pastor of a little country church where in the winter there was so much snow we had to get around by horse and sleigh. It was so cold that the water tank in the kitchen would freeze at night. My clothes would come from a church in Brantford, Ontario, second-hand, some worn out but sent to the 'missionary in Mullingar.' If I had stayed in that place I would never have had any medical help. So for me it is a reminder of God's grace that dad gave up his desire to be a preacher (and his four years of preparation in Bible school) and moved our family to the Ontario to sell aluminum doors and windows.

Because of this move, I was able to get the help of an eye doctor who was a very kind and caring man. It took three operations to straighten my eyes. However, on the way home from the hospital after the last operation, my sister was playing with my toy plane and caught the corner of my eye. It tore the stitches and ruined the effect of the last operation. My one eye would turn in as I was growing up or when I became very tired.

You may wonder why I am hesitant to talk about it. It is because in those formative years kids can be cruel and I remember being picked on or bullied because of my problem. It made its mark on me. I also found it hard to do extensive reading through my growing years, as my eye would turn in.

When I was 16 dad moved our family to Escondido, California, and there I would be shaped by several gifts of God's grace. One was a group of friends in high school who would meet over lunch to pray for our Christian witness on campus. Another was Coach Embry who would prod me to be a witness (sometimes to the guys who would bully me). Then there was my college professor, Bill Bynum. He prodded me; he believed in me; he invested his life in me. He was a gift to me that I did not deserve.

I did not always see my eye problems as a reminder of God's grace. There were times it was a great stress and I was angry that God made me this way. But then I would think how I could have been stuck in the back woods of Saskatchewan with no medical help, if it was not for God's grace.

I had to realize that this eye problem was my thorn in the flesh which needed to continually be submitted to him. This would be my point of discovering his grace. Whatever God would do through my life it would be in spite of my weakness and because of his grace.

While I struggle telling my story I realize that many may have our own struggles with a thorn in the flesh. It may not be physical. It may be a family situation that causes a great emotional burden. It may be a trial of life that leaves us feeling helpless. Yet God wants to step into that difficulty in our lives to show his strength.

My turning point came during my last year of high school. It was not through an encounter with a great preacher but hearing God's voice in an unusual way. My body was growing and I was experiencing extra stress on my eyes that caused my one eye to turn in again. I remember being alone at home one Saturday morning, looking in the mirror and crying over what I saw. I thought, "God should be able to heal me if I had enough faith," so I got down on my knees and pleaded with the Lord to heal my eyes. I got up and went to the mirror and my eye was still turning in.

I got down on my knees again and poured out my heart to God, pleading with him for healing. I reminded him that I believed he could do anything and "would he please heal my eye." When I could pray no more, I went to the mirror and my eye was still turned in. The third time I did this. I read verses from the Bible on how we are to cast our cares on him. I cried. I pleaded, "Oh God, please have mercy on me and heal me. I believe in your power. I have faith in what you can do." I went to the mirror and no miracle.

In desperation I fell on my bed crying. I took my Bible and let it fall open. My eyes fell on this verse: "My grace is sufficient for you for my power is made perfect in weakness."

It was God's voice to me. I read the verses before it, about Paul's thorn in the flesh, how he pleaded with God three times for healing and how God's answered with those words. At that moment I knew that God would not heal me the way I wanted, but he would give me the grace that I needed. And he has.

My church during those years in high school had inscribed across the front of the sanctuary: "My grace is sufficient for thee." I remember how many times I would be struggling, then sit in church and see that verse. I knew it was for me. It was my reminder that got me through my difficult years.

I tell you my story because I want you to realize that your story can also be one of experiencing God's grace. I have struggled with my weaknesses over and over again, but I believe that I am coming to that place where Paul said:

> Therefore I will boast all the more gladly about my weaknesses so that Christ's power may rest upon me. That is why, for Christ's sake, I delight in weaknesses, in insults, in hardships, in persecutions, in difficulties. For when I am weak, than I am strong. (2 Cor. 12:9)

You may have your own struggles with a "thorn in the flesh." You need to decide whether it will be a messenger of Satan to discourage you, to bring defeat into your life? Or will it be a way for God to demonstrate his power in you? Realizing the strength of God's commitment *to* you and his claim that he makes *on* you can help you realize his power through that difficult situation.

Giving him permission to be Lord of all, even of our weaknesses or the hard stuff of life, is not onerous, but liberating. We might be tempted to pray, "I'll go anywhere you want me to go, but please don't send me to _____." Maybe that difficult place is a work assignment, or the cancer clinic, or a million other places is where he might ask us to go because he knows how he can best use us. When we understand the heart of God and how he wants to put us right in the middle of his plan of redemption because of his covenant-making, we will want to cry out: "Here am I – send me!" (or at least timidly whisper).

How is that liberating? When our primary concern is his glory and the glory of his name, then we can trust him with whatever he puts in our way. We do not have to worry if he can use it or if he can use us. He can! Like the children of Israel who were constantly reminded of God's covenant with Abraham or how God was faithful to his covenant in leading his children out of Egypt, our covenant relationship reminds us that God will be faithful to us too.

Chris Christensen expressed this truth in a song with this line: "Till the whole world sees the glory of your name, may your pure light shine through us."[2]

We commit to putting the glory of God on display through our lives because we have experienced a relationship with a covenant-making God.

Lay hold of God, be overwhelmed by his grace and the strength of his commitment to you. Live with a sense of awe at what it means to have a covenant relationship with the Almighty God—the God who is for you, and has proved it.

---

[2] Chris Christensen, song: "May We Be A Shining Light"

Study Questions:

1. Read 2 Cor. 12:7-10 in *The Message...*

    Because of the extravagance of those revelations, and so I
    wouldn't get a big head, I was given the gift of a handicap to
    keep me in constant touch with my limitations. Satan's angel did
    his best to get me down; what he in fact did was push me to my
    knees. No danger then of walking around high and mighty! At
    first I didn't think of it as a gift, and begged God to remove it.
    Three times I did that, and then he told me,
    "My grace is enough; it's all you need. My strength comes into
    its own in your weakness."
    Once I heard that, I was glad to let it happen. I quit focusing on
    the handicap and began appreciating the gift. It was a case of
    Christ's strength moving in on my weakness. Now I take
    limitations in stride, and with good cheer, these limitations that
    cut me down to size—abuse, accidents, opposition, bad breaks. I
    just let Christ take over! And so the weaker I get, the stronger I
    become.

    How do you identify with that description? Have
    you had to face a 'thorn in the flesh' in order to
    experience God's grace? (situation that showed
    your complete weakness)

2. How do the characteristics of God make a difference
    in how we hear his promises or his commands?
    List some key characteristics that would affect the
    strength of what God says to us.

3. What aspect of God's covenant relationship
    encourages you the most?

4. What aspect of God's covenant relationship
    challenges you the most? (most difficult to apply)

REFERENCES

Berkhof, L. *Systematic Theology*. Grand Rapids: Eerdmans Publishing Co., 1941.

Blaising, Craig A. and Bock, Darrell L. *Progressive Dispensationalism*. Grand Rapids: Baker Books, 1993.

Brown, Michael G. and Keele, Zach. *Sacred Bond*. Reformed Fellowship, Inc., 2012.

Dean, David Andrew. *Covenant, Conditionality and Consequence: New Terminology and a Case Study in the Abrahamic Covenant*. Journal of the Evangelical Theological Society. Volume 57, No. 2, June 2014.

Dumbrell, William J. *Covenant and Creation*. Paternoster Press, 1984.

Edwards, Jonathan. *History of the Work of Redemption*. Yale edition,

Erickson, Millard J. *Introducing Christian Doctrine*. Grand Rapids: Baker Book House, 1992.

Harrison, Everett F., Bromiley, Geoffrey W., Henry, Carl F. H. *Baker's Dictionary of Theology*. Grand Rapids: Baker Book House, 1960.

Hill, Andrew and Walton, John. *A Survey of the Old Testament*. Grand Rapids: Zondervan,1991.

Horton, Michael S. *Lord and Servant: A Covenant Cristology*. Westminster John Knox Press, 2005.

Kline, Meredith. *By Oath Consigned*. Grand Rapids: Eerdmans, 1968.

Packer, J.I.. *An Introduction to Covenant Theology*. Fig Classic Series, 2012.

Moore, T.M. *I Will Be Your God.* P&R Publishing, 2002.

Moorehead, W. G. *Studies in the Mosaic Institutions.* New York: Fleming H. Revell Company, 1895.

Murray, Andrew. *The Believer's New Covenant.* Minneapolis: Bethany House Publishers, 1984.

Nouwen, Henri J. M. *The Way of the Heart.* New York: Ballantine Books, 1981.

Saucy, Robert L. *The Case for Progressive Dispensationalism.* Zondervan Publishing House, 1993.

Youngblood, Ron. *Exodus.* Chicago: Moody Press, 1983.

Youngblood, Ron. *The Book of Genesis, An Introductory Commentary* (2nd edition). Grand Rapids: Baker, 1991.

Youngblood, Ron. *Faith of Our Fathers.* Glendale: G/L Publications, 1976.

Youngblood, Ron. *The Heart of the Old Testament.* Grand Rapids: Baker, 1971.

Youngblood, Ron. *Great Themes of the Old Testament.* Harvest Publications, 1968.

Unger, Merrill F. and White Jr., William. *Nelson's Expository Dictionary of the Old Testament.* Nashville: Thomas Nelson Publishers, 1980.

Arnell Motz serves as Dean and Executive Officer of Bethel Seminary San Diego. His teaching area has been preaching, and intercultural ministries. He holds an MDiv from Talbot Seminary, DMin from Westminster Seminary California, and in the dissertation phase of a PhD from Biola University.

He and his wife Terri have served in Ethiopia and Bolivia with SIM, as executive director of SIM Canada and OC Canada, and president of the Canadian Baptist Seminary.

They have three children and four grandchildren.